DIVORCE
and
the
Faithful
Church

DIVORCE

and
the
Faithful
Church

G. Edwin Bontrager

Introduction by
David W. Augsburger

HERALD PRESS
Scottdale, Pennsylvania
Kitchener, Ontario
1978

Library of Congress Cataloging in Publication Data

Bontrager, G. Edwin, 1939-
 Divorce and the faithful church.

 Bibliography: p.
 Includes index.
 1. Divorce—Biblical teaching. I. Title.
HQ824.B66   261.8′34′284   78-4671
ISBN 0-8361-1850-2
ISBN 0-8361-1851-0 pbk.

Scripture quotations, unless otherwise indicated, are from the King James Version of the Bible.

References marked RSV are from the Revised Standard Version of the Bible, copyrighted 1946, 1952, © 1971, 1973.

Quotations from *Divorce and Remarriage* by Guy Duty, copyright © 1967 by Bethany Fellowship, Minneapolis, Minnesota, are used by permission of the publisher.

Excerpts from *The Right to Remarry* by Dwight Hervey Small, copyright © 1975 by Fleming H. Revell Company. Used by permission.

Quotation from *Divorce, the Church, and Remarriage*, by James G. Emerson. Copyright © MCMLXI, by Walter L. Jenkins. Used by permission of The Westminster Press.

DIVORCE AND THE FAITHFUL CHURCH
Copyright ©1978 by Herald Press, Scottdale, Pa. 15683
 Published simultaneously in Canada by Herald Press,
 Kitchener, Ont. N2G 4M5
Library of Congress Catalog Card Number: 78-4671
International Standard Book Numbers:
 0-8361-1850-2 (hardcover)
 0-8361-1851-0 (softcover)
Printed in the United States of America
Design: Alice B. Shetler

10 9 8 7 6 5 4 3 2 1

To my wife,
Edie,
And to my daughters
Andrea
and
Michele

TABLE OF CONTENTS

INTRODUCTION

ITEM: Where once marriages breaking up tended to be "bad marriages" which were dysfunctional, conflictual, and confused, now we see people with "good marriages," by both clinical and community standards, that are choosing to end the covenant.

ITEM: When counseling Catholic seminarians or priests, I find they often look on marriage as a solution to their problems. When counseling Protestant clergy, I note they frequently look on divorce as a solution to theirs. When such ministers are faced with a seemingly unsolvable marital tangle, they not surprisingly think of the solution they've been considering for themselves.

ITEM: Western individualism has concluded that marriage is a contract between two people. When one of them chooses to end it, it is a private individual matter. The biblical view is the exact reverse. Marriage is a contract between two people and the community. Divorce is a community problem. The breakup of a marriage is a breakdown in community.

ITEM: Covenant breaking in divorce is sin, it falls short of God's full intentions for us. Covenant violation by living in a morbid, unloving marriage is sin; it fails God's true intentions for us. Clinical studies clearly indicate that the latter sin is worse than the first in that it damages both children and parents through covert distortion, denial, and dishonesty far more than does the open admission of defeat. Shall the Christian community overlook the socially acceptable sins of carefully concealed yet malignant marriages while courageously confronting the obvious evils of covenants collapsing through divorce?

ITEM: Marriage, as a subcovenant within the covenanting community, is the whole community's concern. When the community oversteps scriptural mandate in pronoucing judgment it loses its authority. When it overextends its grace and acceptance, it loses its integrity. Grace without judgment is cheap approval. Judgment without grace is cold rejection. There is almost no margin of error. If a community cannot find the critical balance point, shall it sin on the side of assuming the right to judge for God or sin by presuming on the freedom in the grace of God?

G. Edwin Bontrager has looked to both the biblical documents and the Christian community to seek understanding and helpful insight for ethical, marital, and communal decision-making. In contrast to available treatments which approach the issue from primarily biblical and theological perspectives, he writes from a communal theology which recognizes the crucial importance of binding and loosing within the body of Christ.

The resources gathered in this book provide a useful base for communities of faith which are seeking to be faithful to each other and to the presence of Christ in their midst while working through the painful decisions with people who are searching for ways of dealing publicly with the private death of marital covenants.

While examining the data collected here, Christian communities must continue to ask the following questions, among others:

How can we blend maximum concern for the spiritual and mental well-being of persons with authentic faithfulness to God's full intentions for us?

How shall we respect both the voluntary choices of community members and honor the moral solidarity of the community of faith?

Can we deal holistically with the problems of marriage and family life without singling out the problems surrounding divorce as though they were more serious than many of the abuses of persons which happen within wedlock?

Are we willing to recognize that the sins which create divorce are committed long before the occasion of divorce becomes known?

Recognizing how little margin of error exists as the community of faith seeks to balance judgment and grace, shall we sin with too much mercy, or sin in severity of judgment?

Can the body of Christ regain its power in covenanting to undergird and support the permanence of its marital subcovenants?

It is the obligation of the Christian community to search for answers to such questions, to question such answers which come easily without painful searching, and to stand with each other in the pain of ambiguous answers.

We are a covenanting community. Covenants are a central concern. *Divorce and the Faithful Church* can assist us in our search to be truly faithful and truly the church.

David W. Augsburger
Lombard, Illinois

AUTHOR'S PREFACE

Judgment-sympathy, criticism-compassion, rejection-acceptance represent the ambivalence of the church on divorce. Churches, attempting to be faithful to their mandate from God, have struggled hard to keep in balance divine law and forgiving grace. Pastors, exiting from their quiet secluded cloisters to give attention to the tumult of men and women bogged down in dead-end marriages, grope desperately for justifiable answers.

Can pastors and their churches share deeply with the divorced, minister effectively to them, and yet remain faithful to their calling? Is it possible for that ever increasing segment of our population—the divorced and remarried—to find in the church pastors and people who are not afraid of them? Do they find Christians who are willing bravely to stand beside them in their defense of personhood? Or do they hear the church saying they have no room for "those people"? Do they perceive rejection in the chatter of those who say, "They knew better!" Do they sense an attitude of alarm regarding the impact of their "bad example" on the young people?

The pages that follow attempt to unravel some of the snarled issues surrounding marriage, divorce, and remarriage which remain entangled in controversy. Divided into four chapters, the book lays a solid base by searching deeply into Scripture, examining what it means, and not only what it says.

Chapter 2 scans denominational polity, directing attention to general variant systems. More specifically these pages focus in upon the principles which denominations today use in guiding their constituent churches in relating to the issues of divorce and remarriage.

The discussion regarding the concepts of law and

grace in chapter 3 shows that living under blind obedience to the letter of the law hinders God's will for us. Grace reaches beyond law.

Chapter 4 deals with practical issues that pertain to accepting divorced and remarried persons as full-fledged church members.

The material in this book was originally prepared as a doctoral dissertation at Fuller Theological Seminary, Pasadena, California. I am especially grateful to Dr. Robert K. Bower, my mentor, who helped give direction and focus to this study. I am thankful also to Dr. Paul K. Jewett of the Fuller faculty and to J. Allen Brubaker of Harrisonburg, Virginia, for reading my manuscript and offering helpful changes for improvement.

Much of the material pertaining to church polity was enriched through personal interviews with pastors of various denominations in southern California. I thank them for their assistance.

A word of appreciation is also due to Mrs. Doris Brubaker and Mrs. Ruby Ludwig for lending their typing skills to assist in the production of my original manuscript.

It is my deep desire that the research and facts outlined in this book will be closely examined and that churches will study carefully their responsibility to divorced persons.

Covering our ears in the midst of cries for help is a gesture of retreat. Inviting all persons to come has always been the pledge of the church that is faithful.

August 1, 1977

G. Edwin Bontrager
Santa Ana, California

CHAPTER I

BIBLICAL DIRECTIVES CONCERNING DIVORCE AND REMARRIAGE

A. Divorce and Remarriage in the Old Testament

1. The Marriage Ideal

Before we focus on the biblical passages that speak expressly to the breaking of the marriage vow, we need to review the institution and plan of marriage.

> Therefore shall a man leave his father and his mother, and shall cleave unto his wife: and they shall be one flesh. Genesis 2:24.

From God's perspective, a marriage is instituted when a person leaves his parents with intent of cleaving to his spouse. In this union they become one flesh. When a person leaves his childhood home he modifies his rela-

15

tionships with his parents and home, and cleaves to another person in whom fulfillment is found. John R. W. Stott points out that in the leaving and cleaving process, a person replaces one human relationship (child-parent) by another (husband-wife). Striking similarities appear in the relationships which Stott sets forth. He says, "Both are complex and contain several elements—physical (in one case conception, birth, and nurture, in the other, intercourse), emotional ('growing up' being the process of growing out of the dependence of children into the maturity of partnership), and social (children inheriting an already existent family unit, parents creating a new one)."[1]

The term "one flesh" is translated from the Hebrew בשׂר אחד *(echad basar)* and comes from a primary root word which carries the connotation" to be fresh, i.e., full (rosy, fig., cheerful)."[2] Probably no meaning can be derived from the words "full, rosy, or cheerful" that would indicate that these descriptions have special significance for this particular relationship, since this Hebrew word is the general one used for the flesh or body of any person.

We understand from this passage that God's intention was that marriage be a union of one man and one woman for life, i.e., permanent and monogamous. Our Savior also confirmed this clearly in Matthew 19.

Marriage was also set forth as being an intimate relationship in which the human being finds its satisfaction and fulfillment. Along with these we see a mutuality in marriage as G. W. Peters sets forth. "Marriage is for mutual supplementation and complementation as expressed in the words 'help meet'—Genesis 2:18."[3] Without the words "monogamous," "permanency," "intimacy," and "mutuality," marriage loses all its meaning and fulfillment. If, for a moment, we compare marriage to a chair and each of these characteristics to a leg which keeps the chair from falling over, we see that each must play its part in maintaining the relationship. When any one of the legs is pulled out, the chair is immediately thrown off balance. Conceivably three legs can hold up a four-legged chair, but there is much more chance of it toppling over with one leg missing. These four characteristics mentioned above are deeply woven into the fabric of marriage.

Marriage was intended to be an enduring relationship of one man and one woman for life. This divine ideal was created and instituted by God Himself. However, even in this early institution of a basic relationship in life, the biblical narrative does not set forth a marriage law. The passage does not seem to be set in legal or contractual terms. It does not say, "Therefore, I command that a man must leave his father and mother and must cleave to his wife . . ." but instead, "Therefore a man leaves his father and mother and cleaves to his wife." The account reflects the natural union of man and woman for their mutual enjoyment and fulfillment.

The concept of "one flesh" brought into focus a complementary relationship. Life became an integrative whole. The "one flesh" concept is taken many times to refer most specifically to the physical expression of sex. However, "one flesh" brings together all the personal components of life. It refers to "two people living together in mutual respect, love, growth, and helpfulness. . . . It is spiritual and emotional. . . . It is more the feeling-flow between two people. . . ."[4] It has to do with both man's spirit and his body.

17

God's divine ideal is that marriages maintain the consistency of this oneness. But with the Fall (in God's written revelation only a few verses away from His divine ideal for marriage) came separation, estrangement, incompatibility and hatred. Before the Fall God set up no provisions in case disruption came into the "oneness" to cause a "twoness." But after sin entered the world a whole new set of complex conditions and circumstances arose. Sin takes its toll. It was inevitable that trouble would befall the most intimate and demanding of life's personal relationships—marriage.

Of the four "legs" of marriage mentioned earlier, we are especially concerned with the "permanency" leg. Jesus indicates in Matthew 19:8, "For your hardness of heart Moses allowed you to divorce your wives, but *from the beginning it was not so*" (emphasis mine). The original intention was the indissolubility of the marriage bond. But now we find ourselves in the disorder of a fallen world. Sin with all its trail of selfishness, mistrust, and brokenness abounds. One must ask, "Are there *now* conditions under which marriage can be dissolved with divine sanction and authorization?" Is it possible that room has been made for God's perfect will to be conditioned by man's weakness and failure? Does the ray of evangelical light we find in Genesis 3:15 apply equally to the disobedience of the first family in eating from the tree in the midst of the garden (Genesis 3:6) and to twentieth-century persons who because of failure in marriage have found themselves caught, trapped, and guilty? Can the church refrain from mediating grace, love, and forgiveness when Christ became that figure who bruised the head of the serpent and brought to mankind the gift of redemptive love?

2. *Mosaic Legislation*

In the Pentateuch we are unable to discover that God expressly laid down a law prohibiting divorce. It seems as though a divine law of prohibition would have been written somewhere within the Mosaic legislation if divorce were to be regarded as an absolute prohibition among Israel. Without question we find even in these early words of revelation from God to man, in the *Torah* (law) as it is called, the beginning of God's grace. We discover this first in the proto-evangelium (Genesis 3:15) as it relates to promise of salvation for all mankind. In Mosaic legislation on family relations, we see God's grace mirrored by His realism as He makes concessions to man's weakness and failure.

Concessions regarding marital relations seem to allow several options for man since he is no longer bound by proscriptions and unalterable law. However, these are not enjoyable to work through. Divorce is always a regrettable development and the process of divorce creates pain and anguish. The Pentateuchal law in the Old Testament does not provide for quick and easy divorce.

a. *Cultural Considerations*

Before we do a specific exegetical study of the most explicit Old Testament law concerning divorce, let us look at the matrix in which the material was written.

Marriage among Hebrews, as among most orientals, tended to be more a legal contract than the result of love or affection. Even though in many cases (as we can see in biblical historical narratives) deep love did exist between married couples, according to W. W. Davies, "in the last analysis it was, nevertheless, a business transaction."[5]

Through the payment of a dowry by the family of the husband, the wife many times was regarded as a good trade, and therefore a piece of property. And so without much difficulty, if the husband were so inclined, he could rid himself of this companion if he did not mind forfeiting the *mohar* which he had paid for her.

This brings into focus the subordinate position of women which was quite prevalent among most nations of antiquity. And yet within the Hebrew economy, wives and mothers were treated with more consideration than women of other lands. Even though the marriage was looked upon largely as a business affair, the wife in most homes in Israel was still the husband's "most valued possession."

However, the husband was unconditionally the head of the home in all domestic relationships. In the matter of divorce he exercised his rights and prerogatives.

The dual code of ethics which applied to the conduct of men over women was another cultural consideration. Polygamy seemed to be permissible throughout the Old Testament period. Thus, a Hebrew might have two or more wives or concubines, or with comparative impunity use any female bond servant in his house for purposes of sexual gratification. According to Jewish law, only when his action involved the free wife of a fellow Hebrew did the full sanction of the law of adultery fall upon him. Further, as pointed out clearly by John C. Wenger, "Women had no such liberties in the Jewish economy. A woman was bound strictly to one husband and any deviation fell under the full penalty of the law. The Jewish free woman had everything to lose by sexual deviation. The bond woman, having already lost something of her dignity, was more prone to sexual promiscuity."[6]

b. *Old Testament Grounds for Divorce*

With this backdrop regarding the Jewish marriage and home, let us make a careful study of the most explicit Old Testament divorce law which is found in Deuteronomy 24:1-4. The KJV and RSV accounts are as follows:

When a man hath taken a wife, and married her, and it come to pass that she find no favour in his eyes, because he hath found some uncleanness in her: then let him write her a bill of divorcement, and give it in her hand, and send her out of his house. And when she is departed out of his house, she may go and be another man's wife. And if the latter husband hate her, and write her a bill of divorcement, and giveth it in her hand, and sendeth her out of his house; or if the latter husband die, which took her to be his wife; her former husband, which sent her away, may not take her again to to be his wife, after that she is defiled; for that is .abomination before the Lord: and thou shalt not cause the land to sin, which the Lord thy God giveth thee for an inheritance. Deuteronomy 24:1-4, KJV.

When a man takes a wife and marries her, if then she finds no favor in his eyes because he has found some indecency in her, and he writes her a bill of divorce and puts it in her hand and sends her out of his house, and she departs out of his house, and if she goes and becomes another man's wife, and the latter husband dislikes her and writes her a bill of divorce and puts it in her hand and sends her out of his house, or if the latter husband dies, who took her to be his wife, then her former husband, who sent her away, may not take her again to be his wife, after she has been defiled; for that is an abomination before the Lord, and you shall not bring guilt upon the land which the Lord your God gives you for an inheritance. Deuteronomy 24:1-4, RSV.

The main difference between the rendering of the King James Version and the Revised Standard Version is that the KJV seems to suggest and encourage divorce in

21

the event ("he hath found some uncleanness in her," the wife,) whereas the RSV merely permits it. John Murray explains further: "In the KJV the apodosis to the protasis expressed in the first part of verse 1 begins at the middle of the same verse and reads, 'then let him write her a bill of divorcement, and give it in her hand, and send her out of his house.' On this rendering, the divorce could well be construed, as mandatory in the circumstance posited."[7]

I feel that C. F. Keil and F. Delitzsch clarify this passage very well, and their interpretation parallels the thrust of the RSV. Regarding these verses, they write:

> Divorce is not established as a right; all that is done is, that in case of a divorce a reunion with the divorced wife is forbidden, if in the meantime she had married another man, even though the second husband had also put her away, or had died. The four verses form a period, in which verses 1-3 are the clauses of the protasis, which describe the matter treated about; and verse 4 contains the apodosis with the law concerning the point in question."[8]

Another biblical scholar, S. R. Driver, says that:

> The rendering of the Authorized Version and the Revised Version is not here quite exact; verses 1-3 form the protasis, stating the conditions of the case contemplated, verse 4 is the apodosis. The law is thus not, properly speaking, a law of divorce; but definite legal formalities are prescribed, and restrictions are imposed, tending to prevent its being lightly or rashly exercised."[9]

In summary then, these verses do not make divorce mandatory nor do they encourage men to put away their wives in such a case. Furthermore, the primary purpose of their writing is not to authorize or sanction divorce.

They rather point out that if a man puts away his wife he must give her a writing of divorcement and if she marries another man, the former husband may not under any conditions take her again to be his wife.

We gather from its introduction in the Deuteronomic code that divorce during this time was practiced, and that it was permitted or tolerated. The Old Testament seems to permit divorce, and when that permission was exercised, there was no civil or ecclesiastical penalty which brought sentence against the one in question.

It may be well to interject here that according to Deuteronomy 22 two restrictions were given regarding a man's freedom to divorce his wife. These restrictions are for the protection of the woman, making it difficult for the man to slander her or accuse her of seduction or unchastity. The first is stated in Deuteronomy 22:13-19:

> If any man take a wife, and go in unto her, and hate her, and give occasions of speech against her, and bring up an evil name upon her, and say, I took this woman, and when I came to her, I found her not a maid: then shall the father of the damsel, and her mother, take and bring forth the tokens of the damsel's virginity unto the elders of the city in the gate: and the damsel's father shall say unto the elders, I gave my daughter unto this man to wife, and he hateth her; and, lo, he hath given occasions of speech against her, saying, I found not thy daughter a maid; and yet these are the tokens of my daughter's virginity. And they shall spread the cloth before the elders of the city. And the elders of that city shall take that man and chastise him; and they shall amerce him in an hundred shekels of silver, and give them unto the father of the damsel, because he hath brought up an evil name upon a virgin of Israel: and she shall be his wife; he may not put her away all his days.

This passage prohibits the husband from bringing

charges of premarital unchastity against his bride. If he took this risk, and it proved false, the man then suffered a threefold penalty—he was beaten, he paid an indemnity, and he forfeited the right to divorce the girl.

The second restriction of the husband's right of divorce appears in Deuteronomy 22:28, 29:

> If a man find a damsel that is a virgin, which is not betrothed, and lay hold on her, and lie with her, and they be found; then the man that lay with her shall give unto the damsel's father fifty shekels of silver, and she shall be his wife; because he hath humbled her, he may not put her away all his days.

In this case, if a man has seduced an unbetrothed maiden, he too must endure the threefold penalty. He pays an indemnity to the father, is required to marry the girl, and loses the right to divorce her. (Further explanation can be found concerning these restrictions in *Hebrew Marriage* by David Mace.[10]) Further, the Mishnah adds three other situations in which divorce came to be forbidden by the rabbis.

Focusing our attention again on the main passage in question, Deuteronomy 24:1-4, the point must be made explicitly that this law was also protecting the wife and discouraging divorce. George Buttrick capsulates this thought well when he says,

> We infer from this law that a man could divorce his wife: (1) only for a good cause; (b) the case must be brought before some public official; (c) a legal document prepared and placed in the wife's hand. These formalities involving time and money would act as a deterrent to hasty or rash action, which end the present law would further serve.[11]

But there was additional significance to this regulative

law. Dwight H. Small, in a recent work, *The Right to Remarry,* gives other reasons for this process of divorce. This really is a protection of the second marriage. He says:

> When the divorced wife has married another, we have possibility of tension. The first husband may wish to get back his wife, and if she remarried in haste, she, too, may wish to return to her former husband. She may draw comparisons and want her first husband back if he will take her. Such a situation could also cause the second husband to go through the pain of jealousy and apprehension.[12]

However, if this Deuteronomic law is followed, all these interpersonal problems are avoided, for the second marriage was to continue. "Instead of refusing to allow divorce, it makes sure that divorce will stick!"[13]

It is interesting to contrast this law of antiquity which seems to show greater civility with that practiced by Muslims yet today. All the Muslim husband needs to do is to say to his wife three times, "I divorce you," and it is legally done.

In this scriptural study I would like to extract certain concepts from Deuteronomy 24:1-4 for further interpretation.

(1) What is the bill of divorcement?

> When a man hath taken a wife, and married her, and it come to pass that she find no favour in his eyes, because he hath found some uncleanness in her: then let him write her a *bill of divorcement,* and give it in her hand, and send her out of his house. . . . And if the latter husband hate her, and write her a *bill of divorcement,* and giveth it in her hand, and sendeth her out of his house; or if the latter husband die, which took her to be his wife; Deuteronomy 24:1, 3.

The "bill of divorcement" (KJV) or "bill of divorce" (RSV) found in Deuteronomy 24:1 and 3 is the translation of the Hebrew ספר כריתת (*sēpher kerîthuth*). The two words literally rendered signify "a document or book of cutting off," according to ISBE.[14] Brown, Driver, and Briggs in their *Hebrew and English Lexicon of the Old Testament* point out that כריתת (*kerîthuth*) comes from the root כרת (*keroth*) verb which means to cut off or cut down. The noun form refers to a writing (i.e., deed) of divorcement in Deuteronomy 24:1, 3, Isaiah 50:1, and Jeremiah 3:8.[15]

It is believed that this bill of divorcement was mandatory in the case of dismissal. One of the purposes served, as mentioned above, was to deter hasty action on the part of the husband. As a legal document it had to be obtained from the legal sources. It was also an assurance to the woman of her freedom from marital obligations to the husband who sent her away. Further, it protected the woman's reputation and well-being, particularly if she married another man.

It is not known when the custom of writing bills of divorcement began, but there are references to such documents in the earliest Hebrew legislation.[16] It is certainly not an innovation introduced by the Deuteronomist.

Later on the Mishnah modified the right of the husband indirectly by making the divorce procedure quite difficult, and "bristling with formalities in ordering, writing, attesting, and delivering the 'get,' "[17] as it was then called. Furthermore, it was considered the duty of the official who prepared this writing to do all in his power to prevent the divorce.

A bill of divorcement would probably read something like this:

On the ____ day of the week in the month _____ in the year _____ from the beginning of the world, according to the common computation in the province of _____ I _____ the son of _____ by whatever name I may be known, of the town of _____ with the entire consent of mind and without any constraint, have divorced, dismissed, and expelled thee _____ daughter of _____ by whatever name thou are called, of the town _____ who hast been my wife hitherto; but now I have dismissed thee _____ the daughter of _____ by whatever name thou art called, of the town of _____ so as to be free at thy own disposal, to marry whomsoever thou pleasest, without hindrance from anyone, from this day for ever. Thou art therefore free for anyone (who would marry thee). Let this be thy bill of divorce from me, a writing of separation and expulsion according to the law of Moses and Israel.

_____, the Son of _____ Witness

_____, the Son of _____ Witness[18]

Another deterrent to divorce was found in the regulations which were imposed regarding the dowry rights of the wife. Throughout Jewish history, practices concerning dowry purchase varied greatly. And in the case of divorce a legal settlement needed to take earlier dowry transactions into account. Even though there was certainly no uniformity regarding the settling of accounts between husband and father-in-law, a fairly well accepted Jewish practice in later Jewish history required that in case of divorce the husband should return to the wife her dowry plus an equivalent sum from his own estate. Thus in some cases divorce might be ruled out simply from financial considerations.

Let me emphasize again that when the husband had found "some indecency in her," he was not required by law to write her a bill of divorcement—this was only a concession to man's sinfulness and not God's answer to marital situations. Jesus later indicates that it was because of the hardness of men's hearts that Moses gave this concession. Furthermore, even when divorce was given, the way was open for reconciliation and return as long as the woman did not form a second marriage. All the machinery of the law and the sanctions of the Jewish community seemed to favor a reconciliation. However, Deuteronomy 24:4 makes it quite clear that once a second marriage had been formed, the way was forever closed for the woman to return to her former husband.

(2) What does "some uncleanness in her" refer to?
Deuteronomy 24:1 says,

> When a man hath taken a wife, and married her, and it come to pass that she find no favour in his eyes, *because he hath found some uncleanness in her:* then let him write her a bill of divorcement, and give it in her hand, and send her out of his house.

The words "uncleanness in her" עֶרְוַת דָּבָר (*'erwath dabhar*) come from עָרָה (*aw-raw'*) which is defined as "to be bare, to empty, pour out, demolish, which has as its resulting meaning nudity—(fig. disgrace, blemish) or nakedness, shame, uncleanness."[19] Brown, Driver, and Briggs defines it as "nakedness of a thing, i.e., probably indecency, improper behavior" and then cite Deuteronomy 23:14 and 24:1 as examples of this use of the word.[20] It is difficult, however, to pinpoint what this specifically refers to. Some scholars have explained these words as referring to adultery. But the Pentateuch prescribed death for adultery, not a mere sending away of the offender. Thus Deuteronomy 24:1-4 probably does not apply to proven adultery on the part of the wife.

John Murray in his detailed research concerning divorce laws in the Old Testament considers Deuteronomy 22:13-29 where all sorts of sexual uncleanness is set forth and concludes that in none of these could the prescriptions of Deuteronomy 24:1-4 apply.[21] And so we find no evidence that עָרְוָה דָּבָר (*'erwath dābhar*) refers to adultery or to an act of sexual uncleanness. As was stated, this phrase עָרְוָה דָּבָר (*'erwath dābhar*) occurs only in Deuteronomy 24:1 and in an earlier passage in Deuteronomy 23:14. But the word עָרְוָה (*'erwath*) occurs frequently in the sense of shameful exposure of the human body as in Genesis 9:22, 23; Exodus 20:26; Lamentations 1:8; and Ezekiel 16:36, 37. In Deuteronomy 23:14 it is used only in reference to human excrement. The "unclean" thing is the failure to cover up human excrement in accordance with the law set forth in the preceding verse. Most likely, then, the "uncleanness" in Deuteronomy 24:1 refers to some indecency or impropriety of behavior. It cannot refer to illicit sexual intercourse, but it could refer to some kind of shameful conduct connected with sex life.[22]

This phrase has been the cause of much controversy in interpretation, especially in the schools of Hillel and Shammai. Shammai, the more conservative of the rabbinical school held the older view, which set forth that only unchastity on the part of the wife could justify a divorce. This extreme view seems to have brought about a reaction in Jewish thought, for the later view tended to extend the grounds for divorce. Thus the school of Hillel interprets the biblical expression to mean any reason whatsoever and cites an example "even if she spoils a dish in cooking"; Akiba adds, almost frivolously, "even if he finds a woman more handsome than she."[23]

The final answer to the precise nature of this "unseemly thing" or "uncleanness" remains a mystery, but it is important that we strike a balance between the rigid interpretation of Shammai (which does not seem to be compatible with other Old Testament law regarding death for adultery) and the liberal view of Hillel. Murray cites Neufeld as saying that "it would thus seem that the phrase denoted some gross indecency, some singular impropriety, which aroused the revulsion of the husband and made his life with her henceforth an impossibility."[24]

We see that the more popular interpretation as given by the school of Hillel broadened the phrase "find no favor in his eyes," to include almost any pretext which the husband might adduce as grounds for divorce. Most likely the Pharisees were reflecting on this interpretation when they asked Jesus, "Is it lawful for a man to put away his wife for every cause?" (Matthew 19:3).

According to Driver, Plummer, and Briggs, the grounds justifying divorce actually set down in the Mishnah are these:

> Violation of the law of Moses, or of Jewish customs, the former being said to consist in a woman causing her husband to eat food on which a tithe has not been paid; in causing him to offend against the law of Leviticus 18:19, in not setting apart the first of the dough (Numbers 15:20), and in failing to perform any vow which she has made; and the latter in appearing in public with disheveled hair, spinning (and exposing her arms) in the streets, and conversing indiscriminately with men, to which others added, speaking disrespectfully of her husband's parents in his presence, or brawling in his house.[25]

And Driver, Plummer, and Briggs, quoting extensively

from above, end their explanation on this point by saying, "It is most natural to understand it as *immodest or indecent behavior*."[26]

(3) *What is the defilement and abomination?*

Her former husband, which sent her away, may not take her again to be his wife, after that she is *defiled:* for that is *abomination* before the Lord: and thou shalt not cause the land to sin, which the Lord thy God giveth thee for an inheritance. Deuteronomy 24:4.

The Hebrew root word behind "defiled" is טמא (*tāme*) which is used of moral, religious, or ceremonial pollution. Murray indicates that "the strength and force of the word may be seen by the fact that when used of moral defilement it can refer to the grossest types of sexual immorality and when used of religious defilement can refer to the gross iniquity of idolatry."[27]

The restriction here in Deuteronomy 24:4 seems very strong and would indicate that there must be some kind of a gross abnormality in the situation where a woman would go back to her first husband. If this would take place, it would be an abomination תועבה (*tōwēbāh*) to the Lord. The passage does not seem to indicate that defilement has to do with the remarriage only; it seems also to apply to the idea of her returning to a relationship with her first husband.

The remarrying of a divorced woman is to be regarded as a pollution or on the same level with fornication, and the law condemns the reunion of such a divorced one with her first husband as "an abomination before Jehovah," because thereby fornication is carried still farther, and marriage is degraded to the mere satisfaction of sexual passion.[28]

Also, just as the bill of divorcement would retard action and a hasty decision regarding breakup, so also would it bring about the realization that there is no chance for returning to the former marital state. Driver comments,

> If the divorce had actually taken place, it would lead the husband to consider the possibility of taking his wife back, while he was still at liberty to do so, viz., before she had bound herself to a second husband. It would also be of value in a different direction by checking, on the part of a woman desirous of returning to her former home, the temptation to intrigue against her second husband.[29]

3. Remarriage After Divorce

According to Old Testament law, remarriage seems to have been acceptable. When one realizes that polygamy was tolerated during this era, restricting remarriage was not a very realistic practice. And the Deuteronomic code says that the woman to whom a bill of divorcement has been written is free to remarry.

However Wenger points out that the Mishnah placed certain restrictions on the woman's right to remarry. This Jewish rule book said: (1) she must observe a three-month waiting period, (2) she may not marry the man with whom she is suspected of having adulterous relations, (3) she may not marry the man who delivered to her the "get" or bill or divorcement.[30]

As noted earlier in the study, remarriage of the divorced parties to each other could take place only before remarriage on the part of the woman. However, the rabbins added five cases under which remarriage of the divorced parties was forbidden irrespective of the formulation of any subsequent union: (1) if the divorce was for suspicion of adultery, (2) if the divorce was on account of religious vows, (3) if the divorce was for barrenness, (4) if a third party had guaranteed the return of the dowry, (5) if the husband's property were consecrated to religious uses subject to his wife's dowry.

4. Old Testament Conclusions

(1) On the basis of the institution of marriage in Genesis 2:24, we see that marriage was to be a permanent union between one man and one woman.

(2) However, as civilization developed, marriages were broken and divorce was happening. We find nowhere in the Pentateuch a law where God prohibits divorce. It seems, instead, that He tolerated and permitted it, and also gave permission for remarriage once a woman received a bill of divorcement. Even though divorce was tolerated, it was not the divine plan of God, but was allowed because of the immaturity and hardness of the people. Also, this particular issue seemed to be surrounded with supporting laws and prohibitions which emphasized its unnaturalness and gross wickedness. Later in biblical history we observe that divorce was below God's intention.

(3) We must conclude that the resumption of a first marriage following a second marriage was strictly forbidden. Again from the later prophetic writings we see this truth set forth. For instance, the prophet Jeremiah says, "If a man divorces his wife and she goes from him and becomes another man's wife, will he return to her? Would not the land be greatly polluted?" (Jeremiah 3:1). This confirms the law of Moses that teaches that to resume a first marriage after the contracting of other unions greatly pollutes the land.

(4) Because women in this era suffered distress as second-class citizens, the Old Testament guidelines provided for their physical and social needs. These laws were designed to relieve the inferior status of women in this culture which left them the unhappy victims of a dual standard of marriage ethics. And, these laws were set forth to discourage divorce by making it difficult and undesirable.

B. Divorce and Remarriage in the New Testament

1. The Gospels—Teachings of Christ

We need first of all to ferret out those passages in the Gospels that speak to the issue of divorce and evaluate their differences and similarities. The passages are these: Matthew 5:32; 19:3-12; Mark 10:2-12; and Luke 16:18. The two longer passages are printed in parallel columns below, with the remaining verses following.

Matthew 19:3-12

The Pharisees also came unto him, tempting him, and saying unto him, Is it lawful for a man to put away his wife for every cause? And he answered and said unto them, Have ye not read, that he which made them at the beginning made them male and female, and said, For this cause shall a man leave father and mother, and shall cleave to his wife: and they twain shall be one flesh? Where-

Mark 10:2-12

And the Pharisees came to him, and asked him, Is it lawful for a man to put away his wife? tempting him. And he answered and said unto them, What did Moses command you? And they said, Moses suffered to write a bill of divorcement, and to put her away. And Jesus answered and said unto them, For the hardness of your heart he wrote you this precept. But from the beginning of the creation God

fore they are no more twain, but one flesh. What therefore God hath joined together, let not man put asunder. They say unto him, Why did Moses then command to give a writing of divorcement, and to put her away? He saith unto them, Moses because of the hardness of your hearts suffered you to put away your wives: but from the beginning it was not so. And I say unto you, Whosoever shall put away his wife, ⌈except it be for fornication,⌉ and shall marry another, committeth adultery: and whoso marrieth her which is put away doth commit adultery.

His disciples say unto him, If the case of the man be so with his wife, it is not good to marry. But he said unto them, All men cannot receive this saying, save they to whom it is given. For there are some eunuchs, which were so born from their mother's womb: and there are some eunuchs, which were made eunuchs of men: and there be eunuchs, which have made themselves eunuchs for the kingdom of heaven's sake. He that is able to receive it, let him receive it.

made them male and female. For this cause shall a man leave his father and mother, and cleave to his wife; and they twain shall be one flesh: so then they are no more twain, but one flesh. What therefore God hath joined together, let not man put asunder.

And in the house his disciples asked him again of the same matter. And he saith unto them, Whosoever shall put away his wife, and marry another, committeth adultery against her. And if a woman shall put away her husband, and be married to another, she committeth adultery.

Matthew 5:32

But I say unto you, That whosoever shall put away his wife, saving for the cause of fornication, causeth her to commit adultery: and whosoever shall marry her that is divorced committeth adultery.

Luke 16:18

Whosoever putteth away his wife, and marrieth another, committeth adultery: and whosoever marrieth her that is put away from her husband committeth adultery.

35

a. Matthew vs. Mark and Luke

The main issue that emerges as we examine these passages is the "exception clause," as it has come to be known, which we will discuss more in detail later. These Gospel writers differ on the use of this exception clause. Whereas Matthew includes it twice, Mark and Luke exclude it entirely.

The fullest report is given to us in Matthew 19. This passage seems to contain everything that is included elsewhere, and so we will concentrate on it.

The exception clause "except for fornication" has triggered endless controversy. As we note the reasons for its exclusion in Mark and Luke and its inclusion twice in Matthew, we shall discover whether these words have more authenticity or less validity, and whether we should give credence to them today. Many writers, scholars, and preachers have for years ruled out all divorce, even in the case where a partner is guilty of adultery, because Luke and Mark do not record the exception. W.W. Davies sets forth a very clear explanation of some of the differences.

> It is a difficult matter to invade the psychology of writers who lived nearly two thousand years ago and tell why they did not include something in their text which someone else did in his. Neither Luke or Mark were personal disciples of the Lord. They wrote secondhand. Matthew was a personal disciple of Christ and has twice recorded the exception. It will be a new position in regard to judgment on human evidence when we put the silence of absentees in rank above the twice expressed report of one in all probability present—one known to be a close personal attendant.[31]

And the writer also goes on to say, "Matthew's record stands in ancient manuscript authority, Greek and also the versions."[32]

Others disagree. William Cole says, "Many New Testament scholars regard Matthew's addition as much later, edited by someone seeking to soften a too harsh dictum. Both Mark and Luke were closer to the Spirit of the Jesus ethic, which was absolutist throughout."[33] Emil Brunner says specifically, "It is my definite conviction, which I hold in common with many other scholars, that this phrase, 'saving for the cause of fornication,' was not uttered by Jesus Himself but that it is an interpolation by the early church, which had already misunderstood the sayings of Jesus in a legalistic way, and therefore needed such a corrective."[34]

b. The Pharisees' Question and Jesus' Response

The Pharisees brought the question to Jesus, "Is it lawful to divorce one's wife for any cause?" (RSV). Very likely the Shammai-Hillel debate regarding the controversial "unseemly thing" of Deuteronomy 24:1 was the case the Pharisees were attempting to try Jesus out on. Shammai took the conservative position stating that adultery and moral misconduct are the only acceptable grounds for divorce. Rabbi Hillel held that all kinds of reasons, even quite trivial ones, were sufficient grounds for legal divorce. E. Schillebeeckx, in his book, *Marriage: Human Reality and Saving Mystery*, is quoted as saying this: "The Pharisees wanted to force Christ to choose between these two schools so that on the basis of His answer they could accuse Him either of laxity or of shortsighted and narrow rigorism, and thus inflame the people against Him. . . ."[35]

However, Jesus at this point did not defensively take sides. He began His answer by calling attention to the original plan of God in creation, almost chiding them for their myopic view of Old Testament law. He questioned them concerning their knowledge of the Genesis account where God made both male and female and instituted marriage as being a one man-one woman relationship. And since this is the divine plan no human scholar, rabbi, or common folk should do away with this sound family setup. This is the ideal and goal for all persons.

But Jesus is questioned further: "Why then did Moses command one to give a certificate of divorce, and to put her away?" (Matthew 19:7, RSV). It is then that Jesus clearly comes out on the side of Shammai and rejects the easy divorce system that Mosaic legislation gave concession to. Jesus replies, "For your hardness of heart Moses allowed you to divorce your wives, but from the beginning it was not so" (Matthew 19:8, RSV).

Another consideration regarding the nature of the text must also be kept in mind. Were the Pharisees specifically interested in what the law of Moses allowed? In this case, as in others, the Pharisees seemed to be out to trap Him. Their intent was to challenge His interpretation of the law. Dwight Small says: "The demand upon Jesus is equally clear: He is bound to answer them in strict accordance with their question, giving neither less than they ask, nor more."[36] As Guy Duty puts it, "The Pharisees had Jesus answer to their question, as presented by them and as understood by them."[37] If all the questions about divorce and remarriage today could fit into this Pharisees' question, which was set tightly in the matrix of the first century and reflected on the Mosaic law as mutually understood by Christ and the Pharisees in this historical context, then our modern-day puzzles could be easily solved. Although addressing Himself to a question on this subject then, Jesus did not, in this situation, bring to us today answers to all the questions persons in our churches are raising. Jesus and the Pharisees were content to stay within the ethical context of the law.

c. Dissolution or Separation?

We now get into the heart of Jesus' response. He said, "And I say unto you: Whosoever shall put away his wife, except it be for fornication, and shall marry another, committeth adultery: and whoso marrieth her which is put away doth commit adultery" (Matthew 19:9).

In all parallel passages—Matthew 5:32, Mark 10:11, 12; and Luke 16:18—the words used in the King James Version have to do with putting away or dismissing one's spouse. Only in the Mark 10:11, 12 passage does the putting away refer both to what the husband might do to the wife, or what the wife may do to the husband.

The Greek verb root used here is ἀπολύω *(apoluō)* which means to loose from, sever by loosening, undo. According to Thayer,[38] it is used in the sense of divorce as ἀπολύω τὴν γυναῖκα *(apoluō tēn gunaîka) to dismiss* from the house, to repudiate, and then he lists all the references which we are using for our study.

Strong's Greek dictionary for the New Testament defines ἀπολύω *(apoluō)* as "to free fully, i.e., (lit.) relieve, release, dismiss, or let die, pardon, or divorce, let go, set at liberty."[39]

Guy Duty, who has done an extensive study in recent years on the subject of divorce and remarriage cites the many original sources where he has studied carefully. He relates that ἀπολύω *(apoluō)* is the exact equivalent of the Old Testament *kerithuth,* which is the word we looked at in the Deuteronomy 24 passage, and he says that it has the same precise meaning of absolute dissolution. He points out that it signifies "to set free; to loose; liberate, radically dissolved; cut loose, as a ship at its launching; discharge, as a soldier from the army; undo a bond; cut apart; to cause all obligation and responsibility to cease; to sever; to free, as a captive, i.e., to loose his bonds and give him liberty to depart."[40]

He encourages the reader to study further the following works for confirmation of this fact: *A Manual Greek-English Lexicon of the New Testament,* Abbott-Smith; *The New Testament in Greek, Lexicon,* Westcott & Hort, 1953; *Vine's Expository Dictionary of New Testament Words; A Greek-English Lexicon,* Liddell & Scott; and *The Vocabulary of The Greek New Testament,* Moulton & Milligan.

Another work, *A Greek and English Lexicon to The New Testament* by Parkhurst, defines απολύω *(apoluō)* as "to divorce a wife, discharge or dismiss her by loosing the bond of marriage."[41]

All these definitions support the view that "putting away" means dissolution, not merely separation. One of the definitions given by Parkhurst is to "dismiss her by loosing the bond of marriage." This would mean that if the bond of marriage is broken, there is not merely separation, but a dissolving of the marriage altogether as in the previous state.

To set forth an historical parallel of this, Duty cites Barabbas. The word απολύσεν *(apolusen)* is used regarding this prisoner who was set free in Mark 15:6-15. He was bound, but Pilate *released* him.

> This bound-released idea is the same in marriage and divorce as expressed by "put away." The power of a Roman governor set Barabbas free. The prison doors opened, his

chains were loosed, and the prisoner was free. So also in marriage and divorce. In a Christ-authorized divorce, the wedding chain is broken and the nuptial captive is released. The marriage law has no further claim on the one released as the Roman law had no further claim on Barabbas.[42]

Also pointed out by W. M. Foley is this: "Moreover it is contended that, when He spoke about divorce, our Lord must have had in mind the complete severance of the marriage bond, since that was the only meaning His hearers could possibly attach to the word."[43]

It seems quite clear on the basis of my study that the word ἀπολύω *(apoluō)* refers not just to separation, but dissolution with the prerogative of remarrying. Lexical works seem to point this out, as do other writers who have done research into the historical background of these verses in which this idea had its setting.

d. The Exception Clause

The exception clause, "except it be for fornication" (Matthew 19:9) or "saving for the cause of fornication" (Matthew 5:32), both King James Version phrasing, is found only in these places in the New Testament. Mark 10:12 and Luke 16:18 do not include it. Neither does Romans 7.

One possible explanation for this is suggested in the *International Standard Biblical Encyclopedia* which says,

> The Scripture doctrine of divorce is very simple. It is contained in Matthew 19:3-12. . . . In Matthew we have the fullest report, containing everything that is reported elsewhere and one or two important observations that the other writers have not included. . . . Luke has put one verse where Matthew has ten. Luke's verse is in no necessary connection with the context. . . . We seem to be justified then

in saying that the total doctrine of Scripture pertaining to divorce is contained in Matthew 19. . . . There is the issue stated so plainly that "the wayfaring man need not err therein."[44]

The reason the evangelists Mark and Luke omitted the exceptive clause in their writings could be that no Jew, Roman, or Greek ever doubted that adultery constituted grounds for divorce. There was no need then to mention this exception since it was understood. Also, Paul in Romans 7:1-3, referring to Roman and Jewish laws, ignores the possibility of divorce for adultery which both of these laws provided.

Let us look next at the original rendering of this phrase. According to the Nestle Greek text, Matthew 5:32 reads, παρεκτὸς λόγου πορνείας *(parektos logou porneias)* (apart from a matter of fornication). Matthew 9:19 reads μὴ ἐπὶ πορνεία *(mē epi porneia)* (not of "for" fornication).

According to Thayer, πορνεία *(porneia)* refers to illicit sexual intercourse in general. It is distinguished from μοιχεία *(moikeia)* which is used of adultery. *The Interpreters Bible* points out that "the word translated "unchastity" is πορνεία *(porneia)*. It may refer to premarital unchastity, or it may also include adultery (μοιχεία —*moikeia*). Hermas (Mandates IV 1.5) uses the two words indiscriminately to refer to the wife's sin."[45]

Some exegetes have held that fornication refers only to sexual sin between unmarried persons, and adultery connotes extramarital relations. We will see later in this book exegetical evidence that such a view is not valid. Friedrich sets forth a wide variety of meanings for this word. It is related to the verb πορνή *(pornē)* and πορνῆμι *(pornēmi)*, "to sell slaves," and means literally "harlot for hire," or "prostitute." Greek harlots were usually slaves. The word πορνεία *(porneia)* itself refers to "fornication," "licentiousness," or even homosexuality.

In discussing the passages in Matthew, the Kittel work points out that:

> In both verses πορνεία refers to extramarital intercourse on the part of the wife, which in practice is adultery. . . . The drift of the clauses, then, is not that the Christian husband, should his wife be unfaithful, is permitted to divorce her, but that if he is legally forced to do this he should not be open to criticism if by her conduct his wife has made the continuation of the marriage quite impossible."[46]

However, at this juncture it is important to discern just what this phrase "unless it be for fornication" really refers to. *Baker's Dictionary of Christian Ethics* cites three different interpretations.[47]

(1) This may mean unchastity before marriage. That is, if fornication which took place before the marital union is discovered during the married state, then the husband may dismiss his wife. However, this does not appear to stand up. In Deuteronomy 22:13 the Mosaic law explicitly commands that in this kind of situation divorce cannot take place.

(2) The "sexual impurity" may refer to marrying a close relative, which would make the union incestuous according to the Mosaic law. Leviticus 18.6-18 refers to having intimate physical relationship with family members. It is doubtful, however, that this is the meaning in Matthew 5:32 and 19:9 since the solution of a situation like this would be annulment, not divorce. The

43

marriage should not have been solemnized in the first place.

(3) This "sexual impurity" or "unchastity" may be viewed as an act of adultery, since, as we shall see, πορνεία *(porneia)* refers to various kinds of sexual misbehavior, and not just sexual sin before marriage. This word may be used to indicate a variety of sexual immorality such as sexual intercourse with an unmarried person, or even homosexuality or bestiality. Since sexual intercourse results in the partners becoming one flesh, there is something about adultery which dissolves the marriage bond. Therefore the innocent party may first legalize the break of the marriage and then may contract another union without adultery on his (or her) part. Or the one who has remained faithful may choose to forgive and to continue the relationship with his (or her) spouse.

Another possible interpretation is that the exception clause provides an exception for divorce, but not for remarriage. However, that explanation does not seem to take into account Jesus' words, "And I say to you: Whoever divorces his wife, except for unchastity, *and marries another,* commits adultery" (Matthew 19:9, RSV). Jesus seems to be talking about when remarriage would or would not be considered adultery. This verse could logically read, "Whosoever shall put away his wife because of unchastity and shall marry another doth not commit adultery."

Nothing in these passages suggests that Jesus Christ forbids remarriage of people divorced because of fornication. He does not seem to reflect negatively upon remarriage in such cases. More will be said about this later.

Another interesting point on this issue is brought out by Richard Detweiler, a leader in the Mennonite

Church. In a sermon on divorce and remarriage, he said, "There remains the point that Jesus would not have contradicted what He says absolutely in Mark and Luke by making an exception in Matthew, and therefore, the exception clause cannot be genuine." But in response to this argument Richard Detweiler commented, "The exception clause is not contradicting to Jesus' absolute statements. It is a modification which recognizes it is not impossible for a marriage to become broken through sexual sin. . . ."[48]

It should also be reemphasized in this context that the Scriptures through this exception clause in no way command a man to divorce his unfaithful wife. Similarly, Deuteronomy 24:1-4 does not command divorce if a man has found indecency in his wife. Forgiveness, acceptance, and reconciliation can take place, and the marriage union can be restored. To hold separation or dissolution as a *command* from God would be inconsistent with the total teaching of Scripture.

e. Fornication and Adultery

The section above alluded briefly to the fact that πορνεία *(porneia)* and μοιχεία *(moikeia)*, both of which refer to immoral conduct, need to be explained. πορνεία *(porneia)* generally is translated fornication and μοιχεία *(moikeia)* has the connotation of adultery. However, these really are synonymous terms and are often used interchangeably. This is also true of other Bible words like "soul" and "spirit," or "kingdom of God" and "kingdom of heaven." The meaning is determined by the context.

The Hebrew word for fornication is זָנָה *(zanah)*. In Jeremiah 3:1 it is used when telling about the conduct of a married woman, and in Amos 7:17 a married woman is a fornicatress זָנָה *(zanah)*. Fornication is defined in *The International Standard Biblical Encyclopedia* with זָנָה *(zanah)* and means "to commit adultery, especially of the female, and less frequently of mere fornication, seldom of involuntary ravishment." And it is also used figuratively in the sense of idolatry, the Jewish people being regarded as the spouse of Jehovah.

Every form of unchastity is included in the term "fornication." Guy Duty compared many Greek word-study helps in this context. He tells us that according to the *Expository Dictionary of New Testament Words*, compiled by W. E. Vine, fornication in Matthew 5:32 and 19:9 includes adultery. Also Thayer's *Greek-English Lexicon* refers to *porneia* as "a property of illicit sexual intercourse in general. Demos. 403:27; 433:25. . . . All other interpretations of the term . . . are to be rejected." And Moulton and Milligan in *The Vocabulary of the Greek New Testament* looked to many times as the "final court of appeals" because it shows from the papyri and inscriptions how Greek words were used in the time of Bible writers, says that *porneia* applies " . . . to unlawful sexual intercourse generally." Duty sets forth much more evidence that *porneia* refers to general sexual sin. Thus it is clear that the words used by Christ in Matthew 5:32 and 19:9 may rightly be taken to apply to the married state. And we need also to keep in mind that the meaning of fornication in Hebrew זָנָה *(zanah)* and πορνεία *(porneia)* in Greek includes incest, sodomy, harlotry, perversion, and all sexual sin, both before and after marriage.[49]

How stringently or loosely can we interpret *porneia?* Is it applied only to sexual promiscuity? It is true that adul-

tery—sexual contact with another who is not one's
spouse—affects the marriage relationship more crucially
than any other offense, and yet there are other situations
that can also make married life intolerable. W. M. Foley
points out that:

> ... This difficulty was met by many of the Fathers
> by showing, on good scriptural authority, that idolatry, cov-
> eteousness, unnatural offences, etc., might rightly be classed
> under the heading of spiritual adultery. . . . There are offences
> which make married life so intolerable that there can be no res-
> toration of affection, that where the tie of affection has been
> absolutely destroyed, the real *vinculum* has been ruptured,
> and that, therefore, such offences may rightly be put in the
> same category as conjugal infidelity in the strict sense of the
> word.[50]

Obviously this is a loose interpretation of the exception
clause, and I am merely raising the issue as to what other
categories, if any, *porneia* could refer to.

f. Adultery—An Act vs. a State

The response is posed by some, "Okay, according to
what Jesus said, it is permissible to secure a divorce when
there is unchastity on the part of one of the partners, but
does that sanction remarriage on the part of the 'innocent' one?" Again, the verse from Matthew 19:9 reads,
"Whoever divorces his wife, except for unchastity, and
marries another, commits adultery" (RSV). Apparently
this carries the meaning, "He who puts away his wife for
fornication, and marries another, does not commit adultery." The implication of the grammar seems to be that
the innocent party may remarry without sin.

However, there are instances when remarriage falls
into the category of committing adultery—for instance

on the part of the spouse who broke the marriage union through the act of fornication. Or one might cite the spouse who seems to be the innocent partner, and who at the first sign of promiscuous behavior of his (or her) partner, begins intimate relations with someone else which leads to remarriage. In essence, the disturbing question relates to whether *continuing* in a second marriage with a former companion still living constitutes a continuing sin of adultery. J. C. Wenger of Goshen Biblical Seminary (Indiana), comments:

> The question of whether adultery is a state or an act compares somewhat with the matter of being married to an unbeliever. Surely that is a state, not just an initial situation when the marriage began, and for a Christian to marry an unbeliever is clearly a sin by New Testament standards. Yet we recall at once the New Testament permission, yes even counsel, to continue such unions with non-Christians where the unbeliever is willing. Does this imply the right of divorced people to continue their unions even when sinfully contracted in the first place?[51]

Another proposal given in response to this question is cited by John R. Martin where he quotes a study paper presented by Howard H. Charles (also from Goshen Biblical Seminary). The paper entitled "Some Aspects of the New Testament Teaching on Divorce and Remarriage" deals as follows with the question of whether adultery is an act or a state:

> Is a married couple, one of whom has been previously divorced for unscriptural reasons, living in a state of adultery? To be sure, they are guilty of adultery. The consummation of the second marriage was an act of adultery against the previous marriage but it was also an act which destroyed the

validity of that marriage. Where the sin that destroyed the first marriage in the inauguration of the second union has been adequately dealt with, it would appear that the second union could be continued without fresh guilt being incurred daily as these two people live together. It must be admitted that this explanation is not a "Thus saith the Lord," and where the Christian conscience can find no rest in this solution, the only alternative is to discontinue a relationship which to them is sinful. In any case, it may be noted that the expression "living in adultery," which we sometimes use, is not found in the New Testament.[52]

Charles takes the position that where the continual second-marriage relationship is looked upon as an act of adultery each time sexual intercourse takes place, then both are living continually with an unpardonable sin. (*Both* because even the partner not married before, according to Luke 16:18, commits adultery if he or she marries someone who was divorced.) If we adopt the rigid interpretation here, then the only recourse at this point is to break off the marital relationship and remain single for the rest of one's life, or go back to the original partner. Or, under grace, is there forgiveness and pardon?

At this juncture it is important to consider the grammatical tense of "commit adultery." It is used in the New Testament in the present tense and the present tense in Greek construction generally means a continuance of the act in question. However, the Greek present tense may also mean an act at a point of time.[53] This allows for the possibility that the adultery committed by entering a remarried state is a one-time act to which Christ's forgiveness can be applied in the same way that murder, theft, or lying is covered by the atoning grace of Christ. A second marriage, then, even when the former partner is still living, may be free from continual sin where there has been sincere repentance and the claiming of forgiveness.

g. Remarriage

Allusions have been made in the foregoing sections concerning remarriage. Briefly, we noted that no declarative statement is given to us about this. The New Testament does lay down fundamental principles upon which we can build. The implication of the grammar in Matthew 5:32 and 19:9 is that the innocent party may remarry without sin.

Obviously there is much divided opinion concerning this. The Roman Catholic Church holds that the exception clause sanctions separation but does not permit remarriage. But, as seen earlier, it is difficult to exclude "permission to remarry" from this clause.

Some may ask, "Why is the Bible so silent on this?" In a sense, its silence is not surprising. We do not find the Bible commanding or legislating on such subideal behavior, as Peters calls it. He points out that the Scripture regulates, forbids, and judges such life instead. Thus we should not expect to find commands and permission for remarriage. The God who promulgates the highest and noblest ideals cannot legislate lower and lesser ideals, though He may permit man to live and to operate on a subideal level. Scripture makes it abundantly clear that God gives commands, not advice. God says, "Thou shalt do this" rather than "It is better to do this." His perfection demands something absolute.[54]

Furthermore, Christ is speaking specifically to questions addressed to Him issuing out of the context of the Mosaic law. Christ was fitting into the legal ethic of the

Pharisees and yet not laying down in these words addressed to them any fixed rule which must be adhered to by His followers at all times in the future. Small sets forth R. V. G. Tasker's perceptive comments in this regard as follows:

> No fixed rules therefore about divorce could possibly have been given which were equally capable of being applied to Christians in the first and in the twentieth centuries. The only static factors are, first, that the divine ideal for the relationship of men and women remains the same, and secondly, that men and women remain the same frail creatures who often find it extremely difficult to achieve in a particular marriage relationship the unity which could alone be truthfully described as "a joining together by God." Jesus, we may surely believe, expects His followers, far from perfect themselves, to recognize this frailty, and to treat it with sympathy; and it may well be that all who fail to do so have not yet fully learned the lesson of the story of Jesus and the woman taken in adultery found in John 8:1-11.[55]

The divine plan from the beginning, then, is permanency in marriage. This seems to be God's law. However, even Christ Himself brings about a relaxation of this law as He relates to a situation of unchastity in marriage which may present itself in the course of living together. He perceives the human situation. Paul, in the Epistles, as we shall see, cites desertion as another factor that may alter the basic ideal. Christ and Paul do not address themselves to all the questions which may arise in the complex area of marriage, divorce, and remarriage. His one main treatment attempts to answer a specific question. To examine what Paul says is the task which lies before us in the next part of this chapter.

2. The Epistles—Teachings of Paul

a. Romans 7:1-3

> *Know ye not, brethren, (for I speak to them that know the law,) how that the law hath dominion over a man as long as he liveth? For the woman which hath an husband is bound by the law to her husband so long as he liveth; but if the husband be dead, she is loosed from the law of her husband. So then if, while her husband liveth, she be married to another man, she shall be called an adulteress: but if her husband be dead, she is free from that law; so that she is no adulteress, though she be married to another man.*

Those who would hold stringently to no divorce—no remarriage come to these verses as a rallying point for their decision. Here it is stated in essence, "*Only* death dissolves a marriage!" However, we need to apply hermeneutical principles here just as we did in exegeting previous scriptural portions. For instance, Archbishop Trench in his *Notes on the Parables* says:

> Another rule of Scripture interpretation . . . is . . . that we are not to expect *in every place* the whole circle of Christian truth, and that nothing is proved by the absence of a doctrine from one passage which is clearly stated in others. . . . For all things are not taught in every place. . . . They came, not to learn its own language, but to see if they could not compel it to speak theirs, with no desire to draw out of Scripture its meaning, but only to thrust into Scripture their own.[56]

However, even in the light of this hermeneutical principle, it is still necessary to do a brief study of these verses so that we may see how they compare and contrast with the other New Testament passages.

First of all, we discover that Paul is stating a general

law of marriage. Second we observe that he is using this instance of the marriage relationship to illustrate the freedom from the law principle which he has been teaching beginning in chapter six. As the death of Christ gives us deliverance from the law, just so a woman is free from the "law of her husband" at his death. The dominion of the law ceased when one who exercised the law died. Therefore we cannot, as Murray says, ". . . fall into the mistake of loading his illustration with more significance than reasonably belongs to it in the context."[57]

Paul in Romans 7:2, 3 is telling his readers about a *basic* principle in respect to marriage. This is a principle as universal in its obligations as the general principle that the law had dominion over man, and had held him captive, until release became available through a new relationship with Jesus Christ. Murray concedes that this marriage relationship is set forth as a binding law that governs the marriage. Yet he suggests that "it should not be regarded . . . as incompatible with this emphasis . . . to conceive of the woman as being relieved from this law of her husband by some kind of action for which she has no responsibility but which involves a complete dereliction of fidelity and desecration of the marriage bond on the part of her husband."[58]

Paul, noting that the husband, by right of the marriage law, rules over his wife, asserts that she is subject to him. However, when he dies, her husband's power over her is broken, and there is no legal connection between them. It would seem to follow, then, that when a marriage is dissolved for the reason of adultery, the "law" of the husband no longer exists.

In verse three Paul is clear in pointing out that if she lives with another man while her husband is still alive, she is an adulteress. The question may come, "Why didn't Paul bring in the exception rule of Christ in the Matthean teachings since it would clearly nullify this hard saying?" It would have been quite extraneous for Paul, keeping in mind the basic purpose of this passage, to take into account the quite abnormal and extreme practice of adultery.

In summary, then, Romans 7:1-3 does not offer much interpretation or explanation regarding the whole divorce-remarriage issue. To take this passage as holding up an inflexible ruling on divorce, and a condemnatory statement on participants of a remarriage is not in keeping with other New Testament Scriptures—especially those of Jesus. A basic principle of biblical interpretation is that Paul must always be interpreted by Christ.

b. 1 Corinthians 7:10-15

This passage of Scripture is divided into two sections with 7:10, 11 referring to a case where a woman apparently was about to depart from her husband, and 7:12-15 dealing with a mixed marriage relationship where one spouse is a believer in Christ and the other not. We will treat these separately.

(1) 1 Corinthians 7:10, 11

And unto the married I command, yet not I, but the Lord, Let not the wife depart from her husband: But and if she depart, let her remain unmarried, or be reconciled to her husband: and let not the husband put away his wife.

First we need to look at who this passage really comes from, which part is what the Lord is saying, and which can be attributed to the apostle himself. The Revised Standard Version punctuation implies that the words in parentheses are Paul's commentary, "(but if she does, let her remain single or else be reconciled to her husband)."

Richard N. Soulen, in an article in *Interpretation*, sets forth the following view:

> Of course, the punctuation itself does not demand that the thought be Paul's, but our contention is that Jesus could not call anger murder, and lust adultery without calling separation divorce. . . . In the parenthesis, then, Paul is speaking for himself and not for Jesus: he commends separation without remarriage as an acceptable solution to an otherwise impossible situation."[59]

As we attempt to understand this passage, we need to keep before us the basic principle, "God's people are not to divorce—it is not God's intention." Small points out, "Yet how different is the tone and form of Paul's counsel! It is not 'cannot' as though an absolute law were being imposed upon all couples in all circumstances. No, the principle of marriage without divorce is reinforced."[60] Paul does not go on to give the exception clause of the Gospels. He is simply setting forth a general rule and does not see it necessary at the time to go into all the special problems which may indeed call for exceptions.

Paul says in this passage that separation should not take place, but if it does, then there must be separation without the right to remarry. Quite clearly this passage forbids remarriage on the part of either spouse. Again, as with Romans 7:1-3, some conclude that adultery gives to the innocent spouse the right to put away, yet neither party has the privilege of remarrying. But there is no indication that adultery was even involved in this case.

Most likely, the woman in verse 11 had obtained a divorce according to Greek law, which was quite easy to obtain, but Paul here is refusing to recognize the validity of this divorce. In her case, Matthew 19:9 with its exception clause of adultery could not be applied. This was, instead, a divorce on the basis of some other reasoning. Therefore, Paul informs her that she must remain unmarried or be reconciled to her husband because the decree she obtained through the courts did not in actuality dissolve the marriage in the eyes of the Lord. If she had divorced her husband for adultery, the case would have been much different.

Let us examine the original language, attempting to understand what is behind the word "depart" in the King James Version in both verses 10 and 11. The Nestles Greek Test in verse 10 renders this χωρισθῆναι (*choristhēnai*), meaning "to be separated," and verse 11 has χωρισθῇ (*choristhē*). Also verse 15, which we shall examine later, has two other forms: χωρίζεται (*choridzetai*) and χωριζέσθω (*choridzesthō*). All these come from the root word χωρίζω (*chorizo*) which according to Thayer means "to separate, divide, part, put asunder," or more specifically in this case, it indicates "to leave a husband or wife."[61] Duty cites Arndt and Gingrich as rendering it "divorce, often in marriage contracts in the papyri. 1 Cor. 7:1, 11, 15."[62]

On the basis of the Gospel writing the Lord would not have commanded the woman in the case of verse 11 to be reconciled to her husband if adultery was involved. Duty points out, "Surely Jesus would not give a woman the right to 'put away' an adulterous husband and then command her to be 'reconciled' to him."[63]

In conclusion, we can say that Paul was "pleading for the claims of honor, purity, and piety in (the marriage) relationship which had been so grossly desecrated in their pagan antecedents and environment."[64] There was no need for Paul in this context to introduce the question of the provisions that apply when the marital relation is desecrated by infidelity.

(2) 1 Corinthians 7:12-15

But to the rest speak I, not the Lord: If any brother hath a wife that believeth not, and she be pleased to dwell with him, let him not put her away. And the woman which hath an husband that believeth not, and if he be pleased to dwell with her, let her not leave him. For the unbelieving husband is sanctified by the wife, and the unbelieving wife is sanctified by the husband: else were your children unclean; but now are they holy. But if the unbelieving depart, let him depart. A brother or a sister is not under bondage in such cases: but God hath called us to peace.

The problem cited in these verses takes another turn again in showing us ethical values in divorce. The problem of mixed marriages was developing in Corinth. When the Corinthians broke from their pagan culture and became Christians, some unbelieving marriage partners deserted and divorced the believer because of his faith in Christ. The question then came up, "What should the Christians do in this case?" Paul responded with a practical answer, and yet one that still leaves questions among biblical exegetes today.

The *Interpreters Bible* states two principles that govern Paul's position (a) The Christian partner is never to take the initiative in seeking a divorce. (b) On the other hand, if the unbelieving partner desires to separate, the Christian is not bound.[65]

Although Paul in his theology holds to the indissolubility of marriage, in this case he takes a rather lenient position. If the unbelieving wife or husband consents to live with the spouse, Paul says, then divorce should not take place, "but if the unbelieving partner desires to separate, let it be so; in such a case the brother or sister is not bound" (v. 15, RSV). A literal rendering from the Greek according to the *Interlinear Greek-English New Testament* for verse 15a is, "But if the unbelieving one separates him/herself, let him/herself be separated." And again it must be emphasized that the word for separation is χωριζεσθω (*choridzesthō*) which is not a word only for separation from bed and board, but divorce.

Along with this concept we need to consider what verse 15 means when it says, "a brother or sister is not under bondage in such cases." Scholars disagree on whether "not under bondage" signifies a dissolution of marriage, and therefore allows remarriage, or whether it means only that the believer is not bound to continue living with the unbelieving spouse, and therefore, is released to enjoy singlehood.

An old work by M. F. Sadler notes that various commentators, even of Catholic opinions, have indicated that contracting another marriage is permissible. He quotes Bishop Wordsworth as saying, "Although a Christian may not put away his wife, being an unbeliever, yet, if the wife deserts her husband, he may contract a second marriage."[66]

Another writer, G. W. Peters, cites Ellicott, Lenski, Robertson, and Plummer along with many other Bible commentators who have arrived at the conclusion that remarriage is allowed in the case of desertion. Peters, himself, then points out some reasons why this kind of freedom can be given: (a) The gravity of the sin of desertion. Desertion is an expression of unfaithfulness and irresponsibility on the part of the spouse who leaves. (b) The emphatic "let him (her) depart." When Christ used this word, χωριζέσθω (*choridzesthō*) it is rendered "put asunder." Man in his sinfulness can put asunder what God has joined together. (c) The words of Paul, "not under bondage." It is impossible to state with certainty that this term definitely means "remain unmarried" or "become remarried." Peters holds on the basis of the relationship of the two words "bound" and "bondage," as used in the New Testament, that more is meant here than just separation. He says:

> Commentators are fairly well agreed that the two words *bondage* (1 Cor. 7:15) and *bound* (vv. 27, 39) have a common root (*deo*) and thus are etymologically related. Therefore, it would seem natural to believe that "not bound"(οὐ δεδούλωται—*ou dedoulotai*)in verse 15 is the opposite from that which is "bound" (δέδεσαι —dedesai) in verses 27 and 39. As the one is bound (in marriage) so the other is unbound (in marriage), thus indicating the dissolution of the marriage bond.[67] (Greek rendering of these words mine.)

The meaning of "not bound" (οὐ δεδούλωται —ou dedoulotai) is "not to be made a slave of" or "not by constraint of law." The word for bondage was a legal term and it meant that persons were no longer held by constraint of law to a former contract. For the married person, it meant freedom from all that the married bond implied. Small offers this thought:

> If a slave was legally declared "not under bondage," his former owner had no claim on him whatever. . . . This is exactly what the bill of divorcement did to the marriage in

the case of 1 Corinthians 7:15. The stronger of two verbs
that could be used here implies that for the repudiated
party to continue bound to the repudiator would be slavery.
John Murray and others who have written helpfully on the
subject would agree with the summary word of Geoffrey
Fisher, "But clearly St. Paul's direction is that a valid marriage may in these circumstances be ended and a new marriage entered into."[68]

In verse 15 Paul says, "For God has called us to
peace." What light does this short phrase added at the
end of this section shed on the subject? It seems to be an
integral part of the thought because in essence it says
that true marriage is peace, and that a marriage in continual conflict is sometimes not worth saving if one
partner is not a Christian. F. W. Grosheide writes:

> If, therefore, circumstances are as Paul describes them,
> the Christian shall resign himself to the divorce. If, due to
> the conversion of one of the spouses to Christianity, peace
> has disappeared in a certain marriage, divorce is permissible
> according to the apostle. This peace is not the same as the
> absence of domestic quarrels: it is an internal peace granted
> by God as a blessing upon a good marriage. If this peace
> would be disturbed by a continuation of a mixed marriage,
> then the yoke of bondage need not be shouldered but di-
> vorce is permissible.[69]

Accordingly, if a non-Christian spouse decided to
leave, the Christian partner was released from the marriage bond. "There is a higher principle than that of
merely trying to retain a marriage contract and living
together; that higher principle is a relationship of
peace."[70]

C. A Summary
(1) It has been God's divine provision from the begin-

ning that marriage be a permanent, lifelong union between one man and one woman.

(2) From the Genesis passage and Christ's affirmation of the creation account, the "putting asunder" of the marriage union is against God's plan and the contracting of another marriage is a breach of God's unconditional will.

(3) The Deuteronomic code which allows divorce does so only as a concession to man's sinfulness, and is not God's answer to marital problems.

(4) When approached by the Pharisees regarding Mosaic legislation, Jesus allows for a dissolution of the marriage union when there is fornication or adultery on the part of one of the spouses, and the "innocent" partner may remarry.

(5) The destructiveness of adultery, however, is not imperative to dissolution, but the divine ideal is that there be repentance, forgiveness, reconciliation, and renewal rather than separation, divorce, and remarriage.

(6) Adultery can be interpreted from the original as an act of sin rather than as a continuing state of sinfulness. Therefore, the hostile feelings and acts which wedged the two partners from each other, including adultery with another party, can be repented of and forgiven. If reconciliation with the married partner cannot be achieved, remarriage is a possibility.

(7) The Apostle Paul, confronted with a Corinthian problem, granted permission for dissolution of the marriage vow when an unbelieving partner deserted his/her spouse. The believer may contract another marriage, but the new union must only be with a Christian.

Our careful examination and exegesis of the pertinent biblical passages has suggested some basic principles we as Christians need to keep in mind in our specific dealings with persons who are personally facing these issues. How do these principles apply to the church today? It is my conviction that where divorce and remarriage have already occurred, the church must be a discerning, compassionate, and forgiving body. On the one hand it must avoid condoning and minimizing unrepentant sin, but on the other hand it must be an agent of Christ's deliverance from condemnation and sin. Both pastoral leadership and laity must search together for the will of Christ in individual cases, attempting to discern through Holy Spirit wisdom what the Scriptures are saying to us and how we can apply them to situations so that persons are lifted up and assisted on the road that leads to God.

We will look at this more in depth in a later chapter.

Notes: Chapter I

1. John R. W. Stott, *Divorce* (Downers Grove, Ill.: InterVarsity Press, 1973), p. 4;

2. James Strong, "Hebrew and Chaldee Dictionary," *Strong's Concordance* (New York: Abingdon Press, 1963), p. 24.

3. George W. Peters, *Divorce and Remarriage* (Chicago: University Press, 1972), p. 5.

4. R. Lofton Hudson, *'Til Divorce Do Us Part* (New York: Thomas Nelson, Inc., 1973), p. 42.

5. W. W. Davies, "Divorce in the Old Testament," *The International Standard Biblical Encyclopedia*, ed. James Orr (Grand Rapids: Eerdmans, 1947), II, p. 863.

6. Linden M. Wenger, "Divorce and Remarriage in the Old Testament" (unpublished manuscript written for a Study Conference on Divorce and Remarriage, April 17, 18, 1961), p. 2.

7. John Murray, *Divorce* (Philadelphia: The Committee on Christian Education, The Orthodox Presbyterian Church, 1953), pp. 3, 4.

8. C. F. Keil and F. Delitzsch, *The Pentateuch* in the *Biblical Commentary of the Old Testament* (Grand Rapids: Eerdmans, 1949), III, pp. 416, 417.

9. S. R. Driver, *A Critical and Exegetical Commentary on Deuteronomy* in *The International Critical Commentary* (New York: Scribner's, 1895), p. 269.

10. David R. Mace, *Hebrew Marriage* (New York: Philosophical Library), 1953.

11. George Arthur Buttrick, *The Interpreters Bible* (New York: Abingdon Press, 1953), II, pp. 473, 474.

12. Dwight Hervey Small, *The Right to Remarry* (Old Tappan, N.J.: Revell, 1975), pp. 38, 39.

13. *Ibid.*, p. 39.

14. Davies, *op. cit.*, p. 864.

15. Francis Brown, S. R. Driver, and C. A. Briggs, *A Critical and Exegetical Commentary on Deuteronomy* in *The International Critical Commentary* (Edinburgh: T. & T. Clark, 1902), pp. 504, 504.

16. Davies, *op. cit.*

17. Isadore Singer, ed., *The Jewish Encyclopedia* (New York: Funk and Wagnalls, 1903), IV, p. 625.

18. Davies. *op. cit.*

19. Strong, *op. cit.*, p. 91.

20. Brown, Driver, Briggs, *op. cit.*, p. 789.

21. Murray, *op. cit.*, pp. 11, 12.

22. *Ibid.*, p. 12.

23. Isaac Landman, ed., *The Universal Jewish Encyclopedia* (New York: The Universal Jewish Encyclopedia, Inc., 1941), p. 578.

24. Murray, *op. cit.*, pp. 12, 13.

25. Driver, *op. cit.*, p. 270.

26. *Ibid.*, p. 271.

27. Murray, *op. cit.*, p. 13.

28. Roy J. Peterman, "Divorce and Remarriage—The Matter of Exegesis and the Question of Hermeneutics" (unpublished study paper prepared for the Brethren in Christ study on marriage, divorce, and remarriage).

29. Driver *op. cit.*, p. 272.

30. Wenger, *op. cit.*, p. 6.

31. Davies, *op. cit.*, p. 865.

32. *Ibid.*

33. John R. Martin, *Divorce and Remarriage, A Perspective for Counseling* (Scottdale, Pa.: Herald Press, 1974), p. 20.

34. H. G. Coiner, "Those Divorce-Remarriage Passages," *Con-*

cordia Theological Monthly, 39, June 1968, p. 372.

35. *Ibid.*, p. 367.

36. Small, *op. cit.*, p. 141.

37. Guy Duty, *Divorce and Remarriage* (Minneapolis: Bethany Fellowship, 1967), p. 69.

38. Joseph Henry Thayer, *A Greek-English Lexicon of the New Testament* (New York: American Book Company, 1886), p. 66.

39. James Strong, "Greek Dictionary of the New Testament," *Strong's Concordance* (New York: Abingdon Press, 1963), p. 14.

40. Duty, *op. cit.*, p. 40.

41. John Parkhurst, *A Greek and English Lexicon of the New Testament* (London: Printed for William Baynes and Son, 1822), p. 59.

42. Duty, *op. cit.*, p. 41.

43. W. M. Foley, "Marriage," *Encyclopaedia of Religion and Ethics*, ed. James Hastings (New York: Scribner's, 1953), VIII, p. 438.

44. C. Caverno, "Divorce in the New Testament," *The International Standard Biblical Encyclopedia*, ed. James Orr (Grand Rapids: Eerdmans, 1947), II, p. 865.

45. Buttrick, *op. cit.*, p. 299.

46. Hauck Schulz, "*Pornei*" in G. Kittel, Gerhard Friedrich, ed., *Theological Dictionary of the New Testament*, trans. and ed. by G. W. Bromiley (Grand Rapids: Eerdmans, 1973), VI, pp. 580, 592.

47. Roger R. Nicole, "Divorce," *Baker's Dictionary of Christian Ethics*, ed. Carl F. H. Henry (Grand Rapids: Baker Book House, 1973), pp. 189, 190.

48. Richard Detweiler, "A Biblical Introduction to the Question of Divorce and Remarriage" (unpublished sermon, June 24, 1973), p. 3.

49. Duty, *op. cit.*, pp. 53-55.

50. Foley, *op. cit.*, p. 438.

51. John C. Wenger, *Dealing Redemptively with Those Involved in Divorce and Remarriage Problems* (Scottdale, Pa.: Herald Press, 1968), p. 23.

52. Martin, *op. cit.*, pp. 22, 27.

53. H. E. Dana and Julius R. Mantey, *A Manual Grammar of the Greek New Testament* (New York: Macmillan, 1927), p. 186.

54. Peters, *op. cit.*, p. 21.

55. Small, *op. cit.*, p. 153.

56. Richard Chenevix Trench, *Notes on the Parables of Our Lord* (London: Kegan Paul, Trench, Trubner, and Co., Ltd., 1915), p. 41.

57. Murray, *op. cit.*, p. 79.

58. *Ibid.*, pp. 90, 91.

59. Richard N. Soulen, "Marriage and Divorce—A Problem in New Testament Interpretation," *Interpretation—A Journal of Bible and Theology,* October 1969, pp. 447.

60. Small, *op. cit.*, p. 164.

61. Thayer, *op. cit.*, p. 674.

62. Duty, *op. cit.*, p. 92.

63. *Ibid.*, p. 94.

64. Murray, *op. cit.*, p. 57.

65. George Arthur Buttrick, *The Interpreters Bible* (New York: Abingdon Press, 1953), X, p. 79.

66. M. F. Sadler, *The Epistles to the Corinthians with Notes* (London: George Bell and Sons, 1891), p. 104.

67. Peters, *op. cit.*, p. 18.

68. Small, *op. cit.*, p. 169.

69. F. W. Groshiede, *Commentary on the First Epistle to the Corinthians* (Grand Rapids: Eerdmans, 1953), pp. 166, 167.

70. Small, *op. cit.*, p. 170.

CHAPTER II

DENOMINATIONAL GUIDELINES
RELATING TO DIVORCE
AND REMARRIAGE

A. Introduction

Even though it is true that all Christian denominations use the Bible as their basis for guiding denominational polity, divergent beliefs on the divorce-remarriage question have abounded through church history. In the first place, the existence of numerous denominations points out that scriptural interpretation on various issues, from modes of baptism to what denotes worldliness, differs widely. The variety of interpretations reflects not so much the question, What do the Scriptures mean? The previous chapter in this book dealt with what the Scriptures say, and what they mean. However, this chapter points out that as church scholars have studied Scripture and have looked at people whose spiritual welfare they feel responsible for, they have not all evaluated these Scriptures with uniformity.

I begin this section by dealing with various summaries that have been made in relation to this diversity and then deal with specific denominations.

Wayne E. Oates, in his book *Pastoral Counseling in Social Problems*, summarizes the attitudes of the Christian church toward marriage-divorce-remarriage under four basic approaches.

1. The Laissez-Faire Approach

This approach involves two extremes. The first is typified by the "marrying parson" who agrees to perform the ceremony for any couple who asks for his services whether previously married or not. The preacher in this case does not consider seriously the possible degree of success or failure of the marriage. He feels that by performing the ceremony, he has at least been in contact with the couple. Possibly their exposure to a short sermon and the sharing of Christian vows will be of some spiritual help to them. At least they will be exposed to more scriptural teaching than if they had settled for a civil wedding.

The other expression of the laissez-faire approach is the legalist kind of minister who says he will have nothing to do with any divorced person. He does not even suggest counseling sessions in order to ascertain the situation. Instead, he holds high the institutional part of his ministry and does not relate at all in this case to the needs of his community, and in some cases, even his church. Concerning one case I personally am acquainted with, the ruling body of the church would not allow the pastor to respond in any way to a couple, both partners previously divorced, who had asked that pastor to marry them. Pastors caught in this narrow bind, impeded by their own stringent convictions or those of the denomination or local congregation, seem to look on divorce as "those peoples' problem."

In either of these cases—marrying anyone who comes along or never getting involved—pastors seem to be either ignorant of the causes and unique problems related to divorce or they do not understand the deep personal needs of the divorce. John R. Martin, in treating this laissez-faire approach, says, "In either case, the approach is basically the same, namely, I will do anything asked of me by a divorced person seeking remarriage or I will do nothing asked of me by a divorced person seeking remarriage."[1]

2. The Idealistic Approach

The approach taken here by denominations or churches contends that Scripture does not allow for the remarriage of divorcees. Even the "exception clause" in Matthew 5:32 and 19:9 does not justify remarriage. In fact, marriage, ordained by God, is indissoluble. However, separation from bed and board is allowed.

Very briefly here, the position of the Anglican Church is set forth as an example. (We will consider their view in more detail later.) The Lambeth Conference of 1930 saw the marriage union as dissoluble only by death. Remarriage during the lifetime of a former partner is unbiblical. The church cannot remarry anyone while a former partner is still living.

As a general rule, however members within the church

are not rejected by the Anglicans because they are caught in this type of a marital situation. Instead, the pastor counsels with the couple seeking marriage. Pertinent information about the couple is given to the bishop for his evaluation. If the bishop feels that each of the members in this proposed new marital union is living in good faith with the church, the marriage is given his approval. However, at this point, the couple is married not by the church, but by the civil authorities, and the church recognizes the validity of the marriage. By remaining aloof from the actual ceremony, the church is demonstrating its stand, and it also feels that it is keeping the biblical standard clear.

The Roman Catholic Church, as we shall see, takes the idealistic approach without the step in the direction of redemptiveness for the remarried couple.

3. *The Forensic Approach*

This approach regards the biblical teachings on divorce as applicable only to a Christian marriage, but not to marriage in general. In this case, the church sits in judgment on the first marriage to determine whether it was a true Christian marriage: hence the term forensic approach.

In this approach, the Roman Catholic sacramental view of marriage comes into focus. Marriage is looked upon as a sacrament for those who are baptized. Again, this will receive further treatment later.

Churches holding this view need to ask these various questions if confronted with a request for remarriage: Was the previous marriage a Christian marriage? Were the persons seeking remarriage professing Christians and members of the church at the time of their first marriage? Since the time of divorce, have the persons become Christians? What about the new union—is it going to be composed of Christians or not?

Two of the problems in this approach are, "How will the theological condition of the previous marriage be determined?" and, "Is true marriage limited only to a covenant between Christians?"

4. The Confrontational and Therapeutic Approach

This is the least judgmental and the most holistic of all the approaches presented. No effort is made to determine whether there is a guilty or innocent party, because rarely is this possible. In a marriage that has broken up, who can say that one is innocent and the other guilty? Everyone involved in a divorce is, to some extent, responsible. In fact, if the partners to this new union were from a church background, most likely the church must share corporately in the sin. Either it provided inadequate preparation for marriage, failed to provide good pastoral follow-up, or lost contact and caring by congregational members when separation took place. Or the breakdown could well be a combination of all three of these.

In the therapeutic approach, the church family attempts to be redemptive by extending itself in any way possible to provide a healing ministry where there are still hurts. This caring relationship which the couple feels from the church goes a long way in aiding each of them in developing a good relationship with the other. More will be said about this redemptive approach in a later chapter.

B. The Denominational Laws

1. A Preview

Before we go into a closer scrutiny of denominational polity, it may help to get a perspective from a little different base than we did from the preceding section. The four approaches discussed earlier actually fall under three general types of church polity—episcopalian, presbyterian, and congregational. In the foregoing we saw a brief overview of the practical outcome. Now we are backing up to see the basis from which these issue.

James G. Emerson, Jr., in *Divorce, The Church, and Remarriage* sets down this nomenclature, and then goes on to treat each of them in greater detail.[2]

The Episcopalian

In episcopalian church polity, power is vested in several levels of authority. An individual clergyman holds the power at each level. A classic example of this is the Roman Catholic Church with its hierarchy. Some other denominations, such as the Methodist Church, have traditionally followed this pattern also.

In considering how this kind of polity relates to decisions regarding divorce and remarriage, we find that one of the individuals in the hierarchy of power is the person who directs the priest or minister as to what he may do. Depending on the construction of this hierarchy, the parish priest or minister may have a highly structured framework within which to operate. This kind of approach gives the minister a maximum of security and limited freedom in dealing with this whole divorce-remarriage issue. If persons who feel they have been treated unfairly want to find a complaint department, the parish minister is exempt. And access to the official may be difficult or impossible.

The Congregationalist

Emerson discusses the congregational approach next so that the presbyterian pattern can be seen as standing somewhere in the middle. Emerson says, "The congregationalist system leans in the direction of no structure at all with regard to marriage. The *Manual of The Congregational Christian Churches* is explicit in stating two principles of church polity: 'One is the entire completeness of each local church for its own government; and the other is the principle which relates to all those duties and privileges which grow out of the relation of one church to another.' "3

In this system, the individual minister has a great deal of freedom. Obviously, though, this system leads into much subjectivism on the part of local ministers of church groups, which in turn results in great differences in the treatment of divorce and remarriage in different churches, even within the same denomination.

The Presbyterian

This system has elements both of structure and of individual freedom. As Emerson says, "It has the problem both of giving too much structure and of experiencing too much subjective judgment."4 More will be said about the presbyterian system within the treatment of individual denominational views.

2. Development

Pre-Reformation

As we have seen, only a few statements are given to marriage in scriptural writings. On the surface, it appeared to the church fathers that complete and unequivocal answers were given by Christ and Paul, and on the basis of these they held to a very conservative view on the subject.

One of the subjects which came up was that of remarriage. Remarriage even after the death of the marriage partner was without exception forbidden to all clergy and generally to the laity, at least during the earliest period. In the third century the strict idea of celibacy came into the church and was institutionalized in the monastic movement.

As one searches through the extant writings of the church fathers, he finds that statements are unanimous in holding that divorce is forbidden except for the cause of adultery, but not all conceded the equal right of sexes in this regard. And there was also some disagreement regarding remarriage after divorce, but most condemned remarriage. Not until the time of Augustine was there a universally accepted doctrine. "Finally Augustine's interpretation prevailed—that adultery is the only scriptural ground of separation: but even this does not dissolve the nuptial tie."[5]

In the further development of church doctrine regarding divorce, we find that Peter Lombard in 1164 set forth in the fourth book of his "Sentences" a clear recognition of the "seven sacraments" including that of marriage. In this sense marriage was thought to confer grace. Even though at first there was some hesitation on the part of the theologians to accept this idea, it was later officially adopted by the Roman Catholic Church and it has remained one of their seven sacraments since the time of Thomas Aquinas.

However, the concept of the sacramental view of marriage brought with it some problems in practical application. For instance, the word "divorce" came to be used in two senses, "neither of which harmonized with its ancient and right meaning as a complete dissolution of the wedding bond" (*a vinculo*, that is, a dissolution of the marriage bond, and, *a mensa et thoro*, that is, a legal separation). However, since no freedom was given as far as a dissolution of the marriage bond was concerned, this expression came to be used to refer to a "judicial declaration of nullity of a spurious marriage which on account of some impediment is void, or at least voidable from the beginning."[6]

On the basis of this explanation and granted liberty, even though final authority rested in the church, divorce *a vinculo* did not quite disappear from canon law. In fact, it seems as though a wide liberty of divorce existed in the Middle Ages, although it existed mainly for those who were able to pay the ecclesiastical lawyers and courts who worked hard, when money was at stake, to dig their way through the maze of forbidden decrees and other seeming roadblocks.

The Reformation Period

With the rise of the Protestant Reformation came the rejection of the sacramental view of marriage. Luther could not believe that grace was imparted in the act of marriage and with it he added the well-known dictum, "Marriage is a wordly thing."

Luther found it difficult to accept divorce for a person who was a Christian but he did give his permission when there was adultery or desertion. There were two other categories where Luther gave his sanction:

> His second view was that, when a person was married to an unbeliever, there was the Pauline privilege about being "unevenly yoked." In the third place, Luther did not stress

74

the matter of remarriage by only the innocent party. The Gospel was silent on that point; hence, by what authority should the church invoke it?[7]

Further with regard to divorce, he saw it as a matter for the whole of society. He wasn't attempting to keep it only within the realm of the church. However, this idea had been universally taught in the Christian world before the Reformation. For instance, in writing on the Sermon on the Mount, he says:

> What is the proper procedure for us nowadays in matters of divorce? I have said that this should be left to lawyers and made subject to the secular government. For marriage is a rather secular and outward thing, having to do with wife and children, house and home, and with other matters that belong to the realm of the government.[8]

Through the Reformation a more liberal and wider interpretation of Scripture, traditional church dogma, and practice concerning divorce evolved. Especially in the rejection of the sacramental character of marriage, the germs of civil marriage and civil divorce sprouted and grew. Dr. Irvin B. Horst, Mennonite writer and scholar, tells us in a paper on "The History of the Position and Practice on Marriage and Divorce in Non-Mennonite Churches" that:

> The denial of the right of the church to control questions of marriage and divorce by canonical law prepared the way for social control through the State. While it can be said that the Protestant Reformation gave marriage a new status and enriched home life, it did this probably at the expense of too great a reaction to the legalistic safeguards which the mother church had set up and with too great a spiritualization of the scriptural teachings.[9]

Even though only two causes of full divorce were granted by Luther and his immediate followers—these being adultery and malicious desertion—many concessions grew out of these. For instance, efforts were made to broaden the definition of desertion so as to give to it a wide range without seeming to transgress the letter of the scriptural authority. Such things as cruelty, refusal of conjugal duty, and quasi-desertion were included. And more extreme theologians like Lambert of Avignon and Martin Butzer went almost as far as modern lawmakers in multiplying the permissible grounds of divorce.

Many differing opinions were aired during the decades that followed the Reformation by persons who George Elliot Howard called the most radical thinkers of the sixteenth and seventeeth centuries. These, to a large extent still appealed to authority rather than to reason and experience in their attempts to solve a great social problem.[10] It was only after about three centuries of struggle that civil divorce regulated by the state has almost universally been established throughout the civilized world.

C. A Treatment of Denominational Views
1. Roman Catholic

In its official position, the Roman Catholic Church has not wavered from nor compromised with its traditional view of marriage as a sacrament and divorce as sin.

To provide some understanding of the basis for the Roman Catholic position, I set forth here an extended quote from a Catholic professor and writer:

Marriage between Catholics should lead to a deep sense

76

of reverence between the partners, when they understand what it means. As has sometimes been said, there are three partners to every marriage contract, the husband and wife and God. It is the third partner who forbids the contract, once undertaken, ever to be dissolved. The same third partner watches over the married life of the other two, is ever present giving His graces when they are needed, and will give His blessing to their common life. Though they now belong to each other and, as St. Paul says, their bodies are not their own but each other's, they both, with their bodies and souls and whole lives, belong to God. Something of a sacrament survives throughout the common life of the partners. St. Augustine would have said that "the sacrament" remains. Certainly the sacrament does remain to all intents and purposes for the marriage bond, which results from the sacrament, remains a permanent means of grace. Permanently, it signifies the unbreakable union between Christ and His church. And permanently it continues to be a pledge of the future union and glory of the married partners.[11]

We understand that marriage in the Roman Catholic Church is considered a sacrament only if its participants have been baptized in the name of the Father, the Son, and Holy Ghost. As a sacrament it can never be un-done—it is permanent. And therefore, logically, it is impossible for a divorce to take place.

Dipping back into history, we discover that there has been from time to time a retrenching of positions. For instance, in the nineteenth century when liberal social movements in Europe were at their peak, Pius IX in 1864 issued his famous Syllabus of Errors. According to James Hastings Nichols, it "was sort of an index of previous papal condemnations, the systematic summary of what Pius thought he had learned about church and state."[12] Among the other condemnations which were made in this document, he said that civil legislation on marriage and divorce was not valid unless it conformed to canon law. In other words divorce in the sense of dissolution, as it is used in civil law, is invalid from the standpoint of Christian doctrine. In fact, natural law, being what it is, cannot accept this kind of divorce.

The Roman Catholic position does grant grounds for divorce on the basis of adultery, but with special definition. The word *porneia* as it is used in Matthew 19:9 is interpreted as meaning a defective marriage. And defective marriages can be annulled. The same goes for the so-called Pauline privilege in 1 Corinthians 7:15, commonly known as "for the cause of desertion." Ramm says, "All so-called divorce cases are reviewed by the bishop's office in each diocese. The divorce is pronounced as a divorce and therefore contrary to Roman Catholic canon law; or it is declared a defective marriage and annulled."[13] Ramm then goes on to explain that if the persons involved are under the impression that justice has not been done, they have the privilege of an appeal to a special institution at Rome known as the Rota. Generally suits of nullity (a declaration of no true marriage) are granted only for grave or serious reasons.

One point that needs to be considered is what the Catholic law says about a "mixed" marriage where only one of the partners is baptized. Credence is given to 1 Corinthians 7:12-15 where Paul allows a departure by the unbelieving partner. Paul here is indicating that if the unbeliever consents to continue to live with the believer, the bond remains. But if the unbeliever desires to depart or separate, Paul says, "Let it be so; in such a case the brother or sister is not bound . . ." (1 Corinthians 7:15b, RSV.)

According to Canons 1120-1124 this privilege is applicable only to marriages contracted by two unbaptized persons, one of whom subsequently received baptism. In cases such as this, the church sees its duty as interrogating the unbeliever with two questions: (1) Do you refuse to "cohabit" with the convert? (2) Are you refusing to "cohabit" peacefully with your spouse, i.e., is there the danger or possibility that you may desire to threaten through attitudes and verbal assault, the faith and morals of him or her? It is also possible, in such cases as these, that the Holy See can intervene and draw up its own declaration. If there is not a desire of the unbelieving spouse to dwell in peace with the new Christian, he may depart. Also according to Catholic writer L. L. McReavy, "the convert is thereupon entitled to contract a Christian marriage, and, if and when this happens, the previous bond ceases."[14]

As stated above, divorce among Catholics has been against church canon. When departure takes place, either because of desertion or fornication *(porneia)* then a separation from bed and board takes place. According to the *Catholic Encyclopedia* the cessation of marriage may have different degrees. "There can be a mere cessation of married life . . . or a complete separation as regards dwelling place. . . . Each of these may be permanent or temporary."[15] However, it is pointed out that temporary abstinence should take place only on the basis of mutual private consent from higher religious motives, and upon deciding this, it is necessary that the partners look realistically at the potential moral danger they are facing. If there is this danger, then they have a duty to resume "married life." Does not the Apostle Paul speak to this in 1 Corinthians 7:5? He says, "Defraud ye

79

not one the other, except it be with consent for a time, that ye may give yourselves to fasting and prayer; and come together again, that Satan tempt you not for your incontinency."

In Roman Catholic jurisprudence if adultery has been engaged in by a married person, the innocent spouse needs to take certain steps before the right of separation is given. First of all, "the adultery must be proven, second, it cannot in any way be attributable to the other spouse either entirely or as an accomplice [I understand this as meaning that the 'innocent' party must have been totally free from encouraging this], third, not already condoned, fourth, not, as it were, compensated by the adultery of the other party. . . ."[16]

Within Catholic law, there is no duty of separation, or even less is there command of permanent separation. It is hoped that love and forgiveness on the part of the innocent party will bring back the guilty one, but there is no obligation, as far as justice is concerned, to receive back the guilty one.

What happens to the party who has been wronged by the spouse and who remains separated? Can he or she finally be divorced? Roman Catholic Church canon gives no option of divorce—hence no remarriage. Freedom for remarriage is allowed only after the death of the other spouse. But within the confines of ecclesiastical life, there is the option, which is encouraged, of entering a religious order and forfeiting any possibility in the future for a reuniting and resumption of marital life.

In summary, then, we see the following features as being salient in Roman Catholic polity:

(1) Marriage is looked upon as a sacrament and, therefore, indissoluble.

(2) The exception clauses in Matthew 5:32 and 19:9 are seen only as allowing separation from bed and board and not permitting divorce. The same can be said for 1 Corinthians 7:15, traditionally looked at as the exception of desertion. On the basis of neither of these situations can remarriage take place.

(3) As a bishop's office in a particular diocese reviews a specific divorce case, the "marriage" has a possibility of being pronounced defective and therefore it can be annulled. In such a case it is said that no true marriage existed in the first place, and therefore the parties can enter into a marital state each with another partner.

It needs to be added that by a recent decision of Roman Catholic bishops a century-old decree of excommunicating divorced American Catholics who have remarried has been lifted. However, full status within the church is not permitted. They may participate in the mass and various church functions, but are not allowed the sacraments of the eucharist or penitence. It is hoped that this step will encourage disaffected or alienated Catholics to seek pastoral counseling to resolve their marital difficulties and again permit them to share holy communion.

2. Anglican

The Anglican laws on divorce grew out of the Roman Catholic statements. For many years in England, the laws of the Catholics were followed, and it was only during the reign of the first Elizabeth that matrimony ceased to be ranked as one of the sacraments. During this time special legislation was required in Parliament to purchase a divorce which allowed for remarriage when the first partner was still living. However, this was very costly, and occurred infrequently.

When the first general Divorce Act was passed for the

Anglican populace in 1857, critics called it "one of the most degrading doctrines that (could) be propounded to civilized man."[17] And subsequent laws were all designed to extend even further the grounds on which a divorce might be granted. In more recent times, one English official, Lord Jowitt, in 1947, maintained that decisions regarding divorce should not necessarily rest upon a consideration of the Christian doctrine of marriage as laid down in the Book of Common Prayer, but rather on a true consideration of the relevant Acts of Parliament.

However, the Anglican Church has been quite authoritative in its ruling down through the years, and only in recent times have the doors been opened for more individual freedom. For instance, at the Lambeth Conference of 1888, the divorce-remarriage question was considered and strict formulations were drawn up which persisted for many years. I will set down the full statement of 1888, and then comment on later statements from Lambeth Conference Reports for 1930, 1948, 1968.[18]

(1) Inasmuch as Our Lord's words expressly forbid divorce except in the case of fornication or adultery, the Christian church cannot recognize divorce in any other than the excepted case, or give any sanction to the marriage of any person who has been divorced contrary to this law during the life of the other party.

(2) That in no case, during the lifetime of the innocent party in the case of a divorce for fornication or adultery, should the guilty party be regarded as a fit recipient of the blessing of the church on marriage.

(3) That, recognizing the fact that there has always been a difference of opinion in the church on the question whether Our Lord meant to forbid marriage to the innocent party in a divorce for adultery, the Conference recommends that the

clergy should not be instructed to refuse the sacraments and other privileges of the church to those who under civil sanction are thus married.

These resolutions were reaffirmed by the Conference of 1908, but an addition was included: "When an innocent person has by means of a court of law divorced a spouse for adultery, and desires to enter into another contract of marriage, it is undesirable that such a contract should receive the blessing of the church."[19]

Another Lambeth Conference held in 1930 declared "that the church must deal with questions of divorce and with whatever threatens the security of woman and the stability of the home" and reaffirmed "as our Lord's principle and standard of marriage, a lifelong and indissoluble union, for better, for worse, of one man with one woman, to the exclusion of all others on either side."[20]

The Conference also recommended that the marriage of a person whose former partner is still living should not be celebrated in the church. However, an exception clause was included here also! They attempted not to pass judgment or make a rigorous statement concerning the practice of regional or national churches within the communion. They also recommended that where an innocent person has remarried under civil sanction, and this person desires to receive the holy communion, the case should be referred for consideration to the bishop, subject to provincial regulations.

A subpoint of their statement focused on the church's responsibility to be ministering to persons, and not only upholding laws! It directed church leaders to remember the spiritual welfare of those members who fall short of the standard. It emphasized the church's aim, indi-

vidually and socially, to call persons to reconciliation to
God and redemption from sin.

Eighteen years later the Lambeth Conference of 1948
contained a ten-page report entitled "The Church's Discipline in Marriage." The report emphasized that the
church needs to uphold the Lord's principle and standard of marriage as being a lifelong and indissoluble
union, but that "it has the duty of shepherding those
who have failed to live up to this standard." It also set
forth the idea that "discipline must not be so rigorous as
to exclude from the church's pastoral care those who
have remarried after divorce. On the other hand it must
not be so lax as to affront the consciences of church
people, or encourage the idea that divorce does not matter.[21]

It also affirmed the position of the 1930 conference
"that the marriage of one whose former partner is still
living should not be celebrated according to the rites of
the Church."[22]

In examining the 1968 Lambeth Conference statements, which are very brief, it is interesting to note their
softened tone. Each conference has shown more leniency
than the one before. Polity has moved largely from the
episcopal ideal to the congregational model.

In Article 23 only five sentences are set forth. Monogamous marriage is affirmed as being God's will and the
only pattern of marriage which bears witness to the equal
sanctity of all human beings. But the article recognizes
that many problems concerning marriage confront the
church. It ends its short statement by saying, "The
Conference therefore asks each province to reexamine its
discipline in such problems in full consultation with
other provinces in a similar situation."[23]

A. R. Winnett in *Divorce and Remarriage in Anglicanism* indicates that almost from the time of the Reformation the teaching and practice concerning the indissolubility of marriage in the Church of England has not been unified. In fact, serious division has been prevalent. Only at the beginning of the present century has there been a regrouping of opposition. In the past the exception clause of Matthew figured high in the controversy, but now, because of the result of New Testament criticism, it figures less. The opposition arose over whether Christ in His teaching was giving a law of marriage, or whether He was just setting forth an ideal or stating a general principle. And if only a general principle, then this necessitated various kinds of allowances for "hard cases" and for human sin and frailty.[24]

Also the question of nullity, i.e., the debate whether an ostensible marriage was really a true marriage, was given renewed attention. According to Winnett, this found its fullest and most precise expression in the American Canons of 1946.[25]

In summary, until recently the Anglican position has been strict in its treatment of those involved in divorce. Within the last few decades, according to the formulations of the Lambeth Conferences, a more person-centered approach has emerged. And yet in many cases the church does not actually perform the ceremony for those seeking remarriage. The church may counsel with them, and if the bishop, upon his evaluation, feels that each of the members in this proposed new marital union is living in good faith with the church, he may give them his approval. But then the couple still is not married in a church ceremony, but by civil authorities, after which the ecclesiastical body recognizes the validity of the marriage. By remaining aloof from the actual ceremony, the church attempts to demonstrate that it is keeping the biblical standard clear.

It needs to be said, however, that remarriage has been allowed in the case of adultery and for the innocent party. This position goes back at least to the eighteenth century.

Possibly the latest word that can be included in this research is by John R. W. Stott who, as a member of the Church of England, comments:

> It is disappointing that in *Marriage, Divorce and the Church* [the Archbishop's Commission Report, SPCK, 1971] the Biblical study is relegated to an appendix and declared inconclusive, and that the report's authors regard their conclusions as "compatible with reason, the Word of God in scripture, and theological tradition" (p. xii)—in that order.[26]

Summarily, he says that the Bible is clear in pointing out that there are two grounds for divorce—adultery and desertion. In both these cases, he indicates that divorce (and therefore also remarriage) are granted reluctantly. If every possible attempt at reconciliation has been made, and has failed, then he feels "we are at liberty to quieten a person's conscience if he/she believes that divorce is the right course to follow. Moreover, *the church should make provision for such people to be remarried in church*"[27] (emphasis mine). This is a liberal step beyond the ruling of the Anglican Church, which has said, "Remarriage means a civil wedding—but the church will approve it!"

Stott believes, though, that some kind of an expression of penitence should be included, even in the public service itself, because every divorce, even when engaged in under biblical permission, is a departure from the divine ideal. However, he says that this expectation from the church that penitence take place is not done "to stand in judgment on the people concerned in any proud or paternalistic way; it is rather to acknowledge the universal taint of sin, as a result of which both we and they stand under the judgment of God."[28]

Possibly through the writings of spokesmen such as Stott and also because of a more liberal trend in the Anglican Church in general, the official polity has been modified even further. Divorce and remarriage are now permitted on the basis of the two permissions given in the New Testament. The church is admonished not to take a standoffish position, as it had in the past, but to take a more person-centered approach.

3. *Episcopalian*

As we noticed at the beginning of this chapter, polity in the Episcopal Church traditionally vests its power in several levels of authority. An individual clergyman holds the power at each level. In this hierarchical situation the bishop does not need to stand responsible for the ultimate decision, but he may turn to a properly appointed court. As he gives his answers, he is speaking officially for the church, and not as an individual ecclesiastical figure.

Episcopal Church polity was taken directly from the Church of England. In 1808 the decision was made to abide by the rules which had come to the American church from England. Remarriage was allowed, but only in the case of adultery, and for the innocent party. The resolution read:

> Resolved that it is the sense of this Church that . . . the
> ministers of this church shall not unite in matrimony any
> person who is divorced unless it be on account of the other
> party having been guilty of adultery.[29]

From this early resolution until 1973 frequent altera-
tions were adopted which yielded no set rule or practice.
Final decisions rested on the bishop, or the ecclesiastical
authority of the diocese, or the missionary district. A
parish priest was not allowed to:

> . . . solemnize the marriage of any person who has been
> the husband or wife of any other person then living whose
> marriage has been annulled or dissolved by the civil court,
> except as hereinafter in these Canons provided; nor shall
> any member of this Church enter upon a marriage when
> either of the contracting parties has been the husband or the
> wife of any other person then living whose marriage has
> been annulled or dissolved by a civil court as hereinafter in
> these Canons provided.[30]

Title I, Canon 18, briefly spelled out the opportunity
for persons to appeal to the hierarchy for judgment and
resolution of their condition. The appeal, however, could
be made only after one year had elapsed from the date
the decree was finalized. And such application needed to
be made at least thirty days before a contemplated marriage. The final appeal, made to a church court, could
take place only if the bishop or ecclesiastical authority
was satisfied that the parties intended a true Christian
marriage.

New polity, however, was adopted in 1973 which
radically changed the whole appeal system. No longer
does the marriage court determine the outcome, but each
case is judged on its own merits by the local parish priest

who has recourse to his local bishop.

Title I, Canon 18, Section 3 sets forth a criterion for the pastor so that he may be guided in making his decision regarding remarriage.

Sec. 3. No Minister of this Church shall solemnize the marriage of any person who has been the husband or wife of any other person then living nor shall any member of this Church enter into a marriage when either of the contracting parties has been the husband or the wife of any other person then living, except as hereinafter provided:

(a) The Minister shall have satisfied himself by appropriate evidence that the prior marriage has been annulled or dissolved by a final judgment or decree of a civil court of competent jurisdiction.

(b) The Minister shall have instructed the parties that continuing concern must be shown for the well-being of the former spouse, and of any children of the prior marriage.

(c) The Minister shall consult with and obtain the consent of the Bishop prior to, and shall report to the Bishop, the solemnization of any marriage under this Section.

(d) If the proposed marriage is to be solemnized in a jurisdiction other than the one in which the consent has been given, the consent shall be affirmed by the Bishop of that jurisdiction.[31]

It is the parish priest who bears responsibility for decisions under Canon 18. Guidelines by one diocese regarding the new marriage canons points out that the bishop can be consulted if necessary. It is this particular bishop's belief that each local priest can make an intelligent and rational decision in respect to his officiating at the remarriage. If he decides to perform the marriage, the priest is asked to write to the bishop stating why he wishes to do so, and sends him a copy of the divorce or annulment decree.

In summary, the Episcopalian position has moved from a rigid legalistic code to a more pastoral person-centered approach. It began with the Roman Catholic position which allowed divorce only after annulment of the previous marriage. Then it specified that remarriage was permitted in the case of adultery and only for the innocent party. A liberalizing trend then provided for church-appointed courts to judge the cases on their own merits. But in 1973 the Episcopal Church gave the parish priest the mandate to assess the situation and make the decision regarding remarriage.

4. Lutheran

Luther's Small Catechism sets forth marriage as the union of one man and one woman for life in the bonds of love and faithfulness. The marriage tie is seen as binding until one of the married persons dies (Matthew 19:6). Except by death, the marriage relation cannot be broken or dissolved without sin against this sixth commandment (Matthew 5:32; 19:9). If one party to the marriage is clearly guilty of adultery, the innocent party is then free to obtain a divorce. No other divorces are allowed by Christ.[32]

As we recall from our historical survey, Luther in his day took a more lenient view than his contemporaries, and we find today in the Lutheran Church in America a position that seems to face fairly and squarely issues involved in divorce. Of those denominations presented individually so far, the Lutherans have gone the furthest in speaking to the real issues in remarriage. The United Lutheran Church in America Convention in October 1956 adopted regulations entitled "Summary Statements on Marriage and Family Life," as a position statement superseding that of 1930. Section six discusses divorce and remarriage:

> Where marriage failure and divorce occur among Christian people, the church should recognize its involvement in the failure and seek to lead all concerned to repentance and forgiveness. If it proves impossible or unwise in the light of Christian love and concern for the welfare of all involved to reconstitute the marriage, then the church should continue, in so far as possible, to minister to each person involved.[33]

Another emphasis by the Lutheran Church is the concept that decisions by pastors and congregations should be made on the basis of the particular circumstances in each case and guided by further considerations such as these:

> (1) We must remember that God accepts the sinner where he is.
> (2) The church has recognized that marriage may be a remedy for sin.
> (3) The church has seen the possibility of remarriage based on Matthew 5:32; 19:9; and 1 Corinthians 7:15.
> (4) The divorced person must do his part in recognizing his responsibility in the breakup of the former marriage, and give evidence of repentance.
> (5) The divorced person must forgive his former partner, and look realistically along with his intended spouse at the obligations he owes to those involved in his former marriage.
> (6) The divorced person must show evidence of his Christian faith and prepare to undertake the full responsibilities of marriage in dependence upon God.[34]

Another of the Lutheran Churches—The American Lutheran Church—holds that marriage is an institution of divine origin but because it is also a social necessity it is subject to the control of civil laws and regulations. It considers adultery and willful desertion as valid grounds for divorce. In addition it says:

> These two "biblical grounds" (based on Mt. 5:31, 32; 19:9; 1 Cor. 7:10-15), however, cannot be offered as a mechanical rule or a binding law, for neither exception is given in Mark 10:11, 12 or Luke 16:18. Moreover, continuing cruel, calloused, or gross selfishness, the very opposite of the divine principle of love, can as fully wreck a marriage as do adultery or desertion.[35]

The church asks that consideration be given to all circumstances involved, and that an evangelical rather than a legalistic approach be taken to the problems of divorce. In the American Lutheran Church, guidelines and not rules are set forth to pastors. With congregational autonomy the leadership is encouraged to relate the divorce cases on an individual basis with authentic pastoral concern.

5. *Presbyterian*

Historically the Calvinist-Puritan tradition, with its outcroppings in America as the Presbyterian and Congregational bodies, instituted civil-law marriage in America. And civil-law divorce followed. Schaff-Herzog points out that the American type of marriage and divorce legislation had its birth in the New England colonies. Whereas in the five Southern Providences before the Revolution not a single instance of either full or partial divorce could be discovered, in the New England States among the Puritans, divorce was quite common. "Dissolution of the bond of matrimony, with right of remarriage, was freely granted [on the basis of] adultery, desertion, and even on other grounds."[36]

The various branches of the Presbyterian Churches, including the Presbyterian Church U.S. (South) which is more theologically conservative than the United Presbyterian Church, U.S.A., take a more liberal stand on this than most of the groups discussed so far. For years they have recognized divorce as a fact of life, have granted the right to remarry, and more recently have permitted pastors to remarry the offending parties after evidence of repentance.

The Westminster Confession of Faith of 1647 was established in 1729 as the doctrinal standard of American Presbyterianism. In 1958, when a merger took place between the United Presbyterian Church of North America and the Presbyterian Church in the United States of America, a revised Westminster Confession of Faith was adopted. Section 6.124 reads as follows:

> Because the corruption of man is apt unduly to put asunder those whom God hath joined together in marriage, and because the Church is concerned with the establishment of marriage in the Lord as Scripture sets it forth, and with the present penitence as well as with the past innocence or guilt of those whose marriage has been broken; therefore as a breach of that holy relation may occasion divorce, so remarriage after a divorce granted on grounds *explicitly stated in Scripture or implicit in the gospel of Christ* may be sanctioned in keeping with his redemptive gospel, when sufficient penitence for sin and failure is evident, and a firm purpose of and endeavor after Christian marriage is manifest[37] (emphasis mine).

Notice that grounds for divorce are allowed on the basis of the *explicit* permissions of Christ and Paul, viz. adultery and desertion, and also the *implicit* allowances of the gospel. However, in the case of the Presbyterian system, the pastor who must deal with the local problem always has recourse to the presbytery—they, then, can in correlating a specific divorce case advise what the implicits of the gospels may allow.

The *1976-77 Book of Order* of the United Presbyterian Church sets forth explicitly this privilege to the pastor. It says in Section 42.31:

> . . . In order to fulfill the corporate responsibilities of the Church to divorced persons seeking marriage, and for their new marriage, a pastor asked to officiate may seek, for advice only, the review and counsel of presbytery or its designated agent in determining the readiness of the man and woman for marriage.
>
> Every presbytery shall establish its own procedure for collaborating and counseling with its pastors in each marriage involving divorced persons. When after this discussion a pastor finds it necessary to refuse to officiate at a marriage ceremony, he shall inform the couple of the church's continuing concern for them and of additional steps they may take if they still desire a marriage service in the church.[38]

Whereas in earlier days the presbytery made the decision for the pastor, today the pastor takes on that responsibility. He knows the situation better than other hierarchical leaders and can relate personally to human struggles with compassion and understanding.

The *Book of Order* also states that the church has the responsibility to educate and counsel before the remarriage. The counseling here deals with the issues of ascertaining the competence of persons to sustain this new familial relationship, and of perceiving how obligations can be met to persons involved in the former marriage.

6. Methodist

The Methodist Church has somewhat of an episcopal structure with a bishop in authority, although in the area of remarriage the responsibility is taken by the local pastor. The *Book of Discipline* makes no statement regarding the necessity for the pastor to appeal to a higher body or to the bishop concerning this issue.

In Section 350-5b of the 1972 *Book of Discipline* of the United Methodist Church, the following guidelines are set forth:

> In view of the seriousness with which the Scriptures and the Church regard divorce, pastors may solemnize the marriage of a divorced person only when they are satisfied by careful counseling that: (1) the divorced person is sufficiently aware of the factors leading to the failure of the previous marriage; (2) the divorced person is sincerely preparing to make the proposed marriage truly Christian; (3) sufficient time has elapsed between the divorce and the contemplated marriage for adequate preparation and counseling.[39]

Article 355c says, "Pastors shall counsel those who are under the threat of marriage breakdown in order to explore every possibility for reconciliation."[40]

This is the only section or article dealing with divorce among parishioners in the 1972 *Book of Discipline*. The questions of "innocence," or "adultery" are not specified in this ruling as they are in the 1956 *Book of Discipline*.

This earlier dictum reads as follows:

> No minister shall solemnize the marriage of a divorced person whose wife or husband is living and unmarried; but this rule shall not apply: (1) to the innocent person when it is clearly established by competent testimony that the true

cause for divorce was adultery or other vicious conditions which through mental or physical cruelty or physical peril invalidated the marriage vow; (2) to the divorced person seeking to the reunited in marriage. The violation of this rule concerning divorce shall be considered an act of maladministration.[41]

The 1976 *Book of Discipline*, however, makes further modifications, providing for less explanation of factors leading to the impasse. It also puts less constraint on the divorced person regarding the intent of the proposed marriage, or the desire for counseling as an aid in averting major problems in the new marriage.

Appearing in the 1976 *Book of Discipline* under "The Nurturing Community," the marriage statement is set forth in the context of congregational responsibility and support. Its position here seems to mollify its severe and forbidding nature.

Article 71—II. The Nurturing Community

(c) Marriage. We assert the sanctity of the marriage covenant which is best expressed by love and mutual support. Marriage between a man and woman has long been blessed by God and recognized by society. . . . In marriages where the partners are, even after thoughtful consideration and counsel, estranged beyond reconciliation, we recognize divorce and the right of divorced persons to remarry, and express our concern for the needs of the children of such unions. To this end we encourage an active, accepting, and enabling commitment of the Church and our society to minister to the needs of divorced persons.[42]

7. Baptist

Baptists make up the largest Protestant group in the United States. They are organized into free churches, with each congregation responsible for its own constitution. Nevertheless, the major Baptist conventions of churches are similar doctrinely. Therefore, certain generalizations can be made regarding their usual position on divorce and remarriage.

John Charles Wynn writes that Baptists hold the basic belief of marriage as God-ordained and enduring until death, but they do acknowledge divorce, and recognize it as a failure on the part of both husband and wife.[43]

But, as in the other denominations, there seems to be a new emphasis on forgiveness for marital failure. We find this in the Southern Baptist Convention as well as in other Baptist groups. Divorce and remarriage are no longer treated as unpardonable sins. However, the traditional restrictions are still common in the more conservative parishes. Wynn writes:

> Some pastors refuse absolutely to perform any weddings of previously married persons. Others will accept only the innocent partner from a union broken by adultery for consideration in weddings of the previously married. Still other pastors accept responsibility for remarriage according to the case; these tend to counsel carefully in the specific situation. And yet a fourth group evidently consider the marriage license itself as the sole qualification; reportedly they will bless the wedding of anyone.[44]

In some Baptist congregations church officers and Sunday school teachers are among the divorced. In certain cases pastors who have divorced are allowed to continue their service in the church, usually after moving to a new charge in another community.

Two groups whose standards and current history are roughly parallel to the Southern Baptist position are the American Baptists and the Disciples of Christ. They have been strongly attempting to encourage uniform marriage and divorce legislation throughout the nation in order to reduce abuses.

8. *Nazarene*

The Church of the Nazarene, composed of 650,000 members worldwide, has traditionally taken a more orthodox and rigid stand on this issue. But in its 1976 ruling some concession is made for persons who are divorced to be allowed as church members.

Looking first of all at this 1952 statement, we find the following:

> (Article 37) . . . The marriage covenant is morally binding so long as both shall live, and therefore, may not be dissolved at will.
>
> (Article 38) . . . We hold that persons who obtain divorce under the civil law where the scriptural ground for divorce, namely adultery, does not exist, and who remarry subsequently, are living in adultery, and are unworthy of membership in the Church of the Nazarene. Though there may exist such other causes and conditions as may justify divorce under the civil law, yet only adultery will supply such ground as may justify the innocent party in remarrying.
>
> #1. The ministers of the Church of the Nazarene are positively forbidden to solemnize the marriage of persons not having the scriptural right to marry.[45]

Another section in the appendix of the above mentioned book has questions that relate to judiciary actions. One question asks:

> #4. A woman marries a man who had been previously married and unscripturally divorced. Would she be barred from membership in the Church of the Nazarene provided her own individual case met the requirements for membership?

Ans: Such a person as that referred to would be barred from membership in the Church of the Nazarene.[46]

The more recent ruling affords a more person-centered and compassionate approach. However, as in the 1952 statement, divorce is allowed only on the basis of the exception clause in Matthew. The exception of desertion offered by Paul is not included. And yet, forgiveness is more prominent, and the acceptance of the remarried emerges more visibly.

Articles 34.2 of the 1976 ruling say:

34.2. Members of the Church of the Nazarene are to seek prayerfully a redemptive course of action when involved in marital unhappiness, in full harmony with their vows and the clear teachings of the Scripture, their aim being to save the home and safeguard the good name of both Christ and His Church. Couples having serious marital problems are urged to seek counsel and guidance of their pastor. Failure to comply with this procedure in good faith and with sincere endeavor to seek a Christian solution, and subsequent obtainment of an unscriptural divorce and remarriage, makes one or both parties subject to discipline as prescribed in 501.

34.3. Though there may exist such other causes and conditions as may justify a divorce under the civil law, only adultery is a scriptural ground for divorce and only adultery will supply such ground as may justify the innocent party in remarrying (Matthew 5:31, 32; 19:3-9).

34.4. Through ignorance, sin, and human frailties, many in our society fall short of the divine ideal. We believe that Christ can redeem these persons even as He did the woman at Samaria's well. Where the scriptural ground for divorce did not exist and remarriage followed, the marriage partners, upon genuine repentance for their sin, are enjoined to seek the forgiving grace of God and His redemptive help in their marriage relation. Such persons may be received into the membership of the church at such time as they have given evidence of their regeneration and an awareness of their understanding of the sanctity of Christian marriage (26.4, 107.1).[47]

The Nazarene position does not specify recourse to a higher board or district superintendent. Instead the decision made must reflect congregational action. According to Article 501 (referred to in the above article 34.2) discipline is directed through a process that includes investigation of unchristian conduct plus a report signed by a majority of the congregation, and filed with the church board. This is followed by a church hearing wherein witnesses bring forth evidence of the charge. Then if a decision receives unanimous support, discipline may take the form of reprimand, suspension, or expulsion from membership in the local church.[48]

9. *Christian and Missionary Alliance*

The Christian and Missionary Alliance Church takes a firm stand in its opposition to divorce. Their official manuals show little change of position over the years. The 1975 *Manual of the Christian and Missionary Alliance* compares its current statements to previous rulings:

We express our unalterable opposition to divorce on any other than positive Scriptural grounds. (Councils 1921, 1949, 1967, 1974.)

Divorced persons who are remarried should not be elected or appointed to national offices or be given The Christian and Missionary Alliance credentials or Christian workers' certificates. (Councils 1949, 1967, 1974.)

In local churches divorced persons who are remarried shall not be elected or appointed to the position of elder or deacon. (Councils 1967, 1974.)

Pastors of the Christian and Missionary Alliance should not perform the marriage ceremony for divorced persons. (Councils 1921, 1949, 1967, 1974.)[49]

10. Church of the Brethren

In recent years divorce and remarriage has been studied and examined thoroughly by committees commissioned by annual conferences of the Church of the Brethren. The study papers that have resulted from these groups in 1964 and 1977 set forth a position of compassion and reconciliation. They offer the church more than an ethical statement, but give guidelines for adequately dealing with such situations with sensitivity and understanding. The statements encourage creative ministry to persons reaching for help during traumatic marital crises.

The 1964 report first set forth the intent of God that the marriage relationship be lifelong and indissoluble. But God's perfect will is denied by His creatures, and the church is entrusted with a ministry of reconciliation and healing. However, it is recognized that broken relationships sometimes pass a point of no return, and divorce seems to be the only alternative.

Unfaithfulness, both in the act of adultery, and in other ways, can destroy a marriage. From the earliest days of Christianity, the use of the "exceptive clause" (Matthew 19:9 and 5:32) and the teaching of Paul in 1 Corinthians 7 led the church to recognize that not all marriages, even of persons who are members of the church, were truly ordained of God.[50]

The 1964 committee felt that the church's traditional stand on the remarriage of divorced persons, which persisted from the 1933 Annual Conference Minutes, must be reappraised. This read, "Ordained ministers performing marriage ceremonies should exercise care not to officiate at weddings where the contract parties have one or more living companions. . . ."[51]

The 1964 report recommended a position which allowed for remarriage:

Furthermore, we believe that the church, in further applying the Spirit of Christ to the current situation, is challenged to take the following steps:

1. To maintain as the Christian standard the concept of marriage as divinely willed, lifelong, monogamous, and indissoluble.

2. To seek without reservation to restore the relationships when its unity has been damaged or destroyed through sin of whatever variety.

3. To recognize that under some circumstances this redemptive approach may include divorce as a means of resolving the former bond, and the freedom to enter a new marriage with the guidance and blessing of the church.

4. When persons who have been divorced seek to be remarried to each other, or to other persons, ministers of the Church of the Brethren may be permitted to perform such marriages under the following conditions:

(a). The person who has been divorced shows evidence of penitence for his or her own responsibility in the failure of the former marriage.

(b). Both parties to the proposed marriage show evidence that they are seeking a mature understanding of and commitment to the standards of true Christian marriage.

(c). Such marriage may be performed only if the pastor will have the opportunity for continued pastoral guidance of the couple.

(d). It should be understood that it is not the practice of the church and its ministers, in every case, to accede to the request for the solemnization of the marriage of divorced persons, but only in those instances wherein the above conditions are fulfilled; and that no minister of the church, against his own conscience, is obliged to marry a couple of which one or both persons have been divorced.[52]

The 1977 report of the committee assigned to assist the Church of the Brethren in reassessing the 1964 position sets forth a reaffirmation of this position regarding remarriage. The 1964 statement gave freedom to persons "to enter a new marriage with the guidance and blessing of the church." In reaffirming this position the committee said. "We . . . urge members of the church to be loving rather than judgmental with regard to remarriage, both of laity and the clergy."[53]

The 1977 position paper adopted by the delegate body in Richmond, Virginia, includes excellent suggestions for divorce and remarriage counseling. It provides assistance for creative action by the local congregation in reaching out with arms of love rather than pulling away because of minds filled with judgment.

The Church of the Brethren position offers tolerance when an impasse in marital conflict appears. But better yet, it provides a wealth of ideas and suggestions that, if used by the local congregation, will restrain and curb unmanageable marriage problems.

11. Mennonite

As with other congregationally governed churches, there has not been a uniform practice throughout Mennonite history regarding divorce and remarriage nor is there uniformity within the polity of the Mennonite Church today.

Menno Simons, the sixteenth-century Dutch Anabaptist leader from whom Mennonites derive their name, described his understanding of marriage thus:

We acknowledge, teach, and assent to no other marriage than that which Christ and His apostles publicly and plainly taught in the New Testament, namely, one man and one woman (Matthew 19:4), and that they may not be divorced except in case of adultery (Matthew 5:32); for the two are one flesh, but if the unbelieving one depart, a sister or brother is not under bondage in that case (1 Corinthians 7:15).[54]

Article IV of the Wismar Articles of 1554 contained in the same work as the above, says:

In the fourth place, if a believer and an unbeliever are in the marriage bond together and the unbeliever commits adultery, then the marriage tie is broken. And if it be one who complains that he has fallen in sin, and desires to mend his ways, then the brethren permit the believing mate to go to the unfaithful one to admonish him, if conscience allows it in view of the state of the affair. But if he be a bold and headstrong adulterer, then the innocent party is free—with the provision, however, that she shall consult with the congregation and remarry according to circumstances and decisions in that matter, be it well understood.[55]

A rigid view was taken from 1690 to 1800. In the latter part of the 1800s various district conferences faced the divorce-remarriage issue, and a more redemptive attitude was extended again by the brotherhood to persons having this kind of marital difficulty.

J. C. Wenger summarizes the principles the Mennonite Church seemed to follow in the latter decades of the nineteenth century:

It is thus evident that the prevailing view in the Mennonite Church in the latter decades of the nineteenth century was that marriage ought to be permanent. But where lives were broken by sin, and people were divorced and remarried legally, and the Spirit of God then brought them to repentance and faith; our brotherhood then stretched out to them a welcoming hand and received them as members, in spite of the sins of the past. Our church then followed the principle, whatever one's state was when he was called of God, let him abide in that state (1 Corinthians 7:17, 20, 24).[56]

However, during the first half of the twentieth century, through the biblical interpretation of various strong leaders within the church, a very restricted view was advocated again on the divorce question.

The current understanding of divorce-remarriage issues is quite varied within the Mennonite Church. Many local congregations, for whom the issues are no longer academic, are looking anew for answers and are arriving at various conclusions. And larger bodies such as district conferences have not reached a uniform conclusion.

John R. Martin, in discussing the historical Mennonite perspectives on the issues, sets forth four summary statements which show in general where the Mennonite Church stands:

(1) Christian marriage is understood to involve man, woman, and God focusing on a commitment of faithfulness for life.

(2) While unfaithfulness or adultery does not dissolve the marriage requiring separation or divorce, it does severely strain the marriage union and may cause separation or divorce.

(3) When persons apply for membership who are remarried with their first partner still living, approval of the congregation is required before membership is extended. Some congregations would not grant membership privileges regardless of background circumstances while others would do so on a selective basis such as divorce due to adultery or

divorce and remarriage prior to conversion.

(4) The attitude of the church toward believers or members involved in divorce and remarriage is quite varied. In some congregations they lose their membership. In other congregations membership is retained. This urgent problem needs an answer today.[57]

Since doctrine is not handed down by some hierarchical body in the Mennonite Church, congregations who have been realistic about the strains on marriage in our contemporary culture have done scriptural and historical studies and have issued recommendations.

The Trinity Mennonite Church, Glendale, Arizona, is one example of this. In dealing with the remarriage of persons, both of whom had been divorced, the church drew up a procedure for studying the issues. The couple was also present in the discussions which followed.

The procedure for arriving at a congregational decision regarding divorce and remarriage was stated by the board of elders of the Trinity Church as follows:

(1) We believe that the Scripture teaches that Christian marriage is to be a lifelong relationship of one man and one woman.

(2) We believe that the grace of God is able to save any lost person and to forgive all persons of every sin except the blasphemy of the Holy Spirit.

(3) We believe that as children of God we must be biblical, redemptive, forgiving, nonjudgmental in our attitude towards all persons, and Christlike in our spirit.

(4) We ask that every member make this a matter of personal concern and daily prayer.

(5) We ask that our love and concern be further expressed by refraining from any and all gossip, and to refrain from discussing this matter with anyone outside our congregation.

(6) We ask that everyone show a genuine Christian spirit toward all persons concerned. This is a time of deep searching and concern for each person.

(7) We ask that each member be present at all called members meetings regarding this matter, share your convictions in Christian love, give and receive counsel, and work together in the spirit of Christ and in the unity of the Holy Spirit.

(8) We ask that you study the following Scriptures openly and prayerfully *on marriage, divorce, and remarriage*;

a. Genesis 1:26-28; 2:18-24	g. Luke 16:18
b. Exodus 20:14	h. John 8:2-11
c. Deuteronomy 24:1-4	i. 1 Corinthians 7:1-40
d. Matthew 5:27-32	j. Ephesians 5:21-23
e. Matthew 19:1-12	k. Colossians 3:18, 19
f. Mark 10:1-12	l. 1 Peter 3:1-7

(9) Let us remember that we are called to be a caring, forgiving fellowship and to be a discerning brotherhood faithful to God and His Word.

After several weeks of Bible study and discussion the congregation made a decision, not by majority vote, but by consensus. They decided that the factors pertaining to this case did not call for rejection. Instead forgiveness, love, and acceptance were necessary. Therefore the couple was remarried and assimilated into full fellowship within the brotherhood.

Working through a decision on the basis of such a plan means that each case must be looked at on its own individual merits. The decision is not made on the basis of a blanket statement.

A recent statistical study of Mennonite practice and belief researched by Kauffman and Harder revealed a changing attitude among church members toward the divorced and remarried:

These findings suggest that the most common position of present-day church members is to accept the divorced and remarried person on the basis of confession and forgiveness. At least one fourth would support an even more liberal position. Given the present flux of attitudes and the tendency of official denominational policy to be restudied and possibly altered, and given the small but increasing number of couples who divorce and remarry but at the same time seek to retain their fellowship with their congregations, it is possible that the rule against acceptance of divorced and remarried persons will be relaxed.[58]

D. A Summary

As we reflect on both the Roman Catholic and Protestant traditions of church life, there seems to be much stirring these days on the divorce-remarriage issue. Even in Catholic circles, books are being written which cry out for more leniency and less law. In some places the divorced are finding new grace which is being brought to them on the basis of more openness of canon law.

We have noted that a majority of Protestant denominations have been moving away from legalistic standards toward a new emphasis on reconciliation and forgiveness. Divorce is being considered less the unpardonable sin and more in the category of man's other failures.

Pastors and many congregational members are sensing a deeper concern for persons and their family relationships and are laying less stress on impersonal and inflexible regulations. Perhaps this attitude is traced to the fact that more exposure to the divorced person's trauma evokes more response.

In churches where divorce seems to be the worst taboo, marital problems are often deeply buried and do not come before the congregation for help. But where deep problems are revealed, congregational friends can more easily make a transition from being coldly detached to becoming warmly compassionate. In fact, a decreased stigma on marital difficulties within the church may prompt couples to find help from a friend, marriage counselor, or pastor before they have reached a point of no return. Greater exposure may assist in saving marriages whereas concealment of the problem may cause an internal divorce even though spiritual conviction deters legal divorce.

No doubt, societal conditions have evoked greater exposure. Couples have realized that they are not the only persons caught in despair, and therefore they have begun inquiring for help, not fearing degradation by peers. Churches, sensing more marital difficulties, have moved closer to these issues, and as a consequence are ministering to people's individual needs. This, in turn, has resulted in the practice of less law and more grace and compassion.

Another summarization can be made regarding where the decisions seem more to be resting. In the more evangelical and conservative congregations, but also in some mainline groups, more responsibility is being placed on the local congregation and pastor. Being closer to the situation, this approach encourages sensitivity to an individual's plight. But allowing each local congregation or district to arrive at its own conclusion also has its shortcomings. In the smaller bodies, parishioners look to the pastor as the Bible scholar and interpreter, and if the pastor holds to a narrow view of Scripture he can force the people to accept his line of thinking.

Bernard Ramm reflects on a desirable stance for the church to take today:

Therefore our Protestant Churches need a new sense of compassion, a new sense of mercy, a new sense of redemption, and need to make a real effort at understanding the tragedy of divorce. Every effort should be made to redeem these people, and open up doors of hope for them rather than plunging them into deeper despair or deeper problems.[59]

The Christian church today must rediscover its call of ministry to men and women everywhere in our secular age, remembering that their needs are not only spiritual and physical, but also social and psychological. Not to minister to those caught in the web of divorce is to limit Christ's commission to less than two thirds of the married or formerly married persons living around us!

Notes: Chapter II

1. John R. Martin, *Divorce and Remarriage, A Perspective for Counseling* (Scottdale, Pa.: Herald Press, 1974), p. 25.

2. James G. Emerson, Jr., *Divorce, the Church, and Remarriage* (Philadelphia: Westminster Press, 1952), pp. 109-147.

3. *Ibid.*, p. 110.

4. *Ibid.*, p. 111.

5. George Elliott Howard, "Divorce," *Schaff-Herzog Encyclopedia of Religious Knowledge*, ed. Samuel Macauley Jackson (New York: Funk and Wagnalls, 1891), III, p. 452.

6. *Ibid.*

7. Emerson, *op. cit.*, p. 106.

8. *Ibid.*, p. 106, Gibson Winter quoting Luther in an unpublished paper for the office of Family Education Research of the Board of Christian Education of the United Presbyterian Church in the U.S.A.

9. Irvin B. Horst, "The History of the Position and Practice on Marriage and Divorce in Non-Mennonite Churches" (unpublished manuscript written for the Study Conference on Divorce and Remarriage, April 17, 18, 1961), pp. 4, 5.

10. Howard, *op. cit.*, p. 454.

11. H. F. Davis, "Marriage as a Sacrament," *Catholics and Di-*

vorce, ed. Patrick J. O'Mahoney (London: Thomas Nelson and Sons, 1959), p. 27.

12. James Hastings Nichols, *History of Christianity, 1650-1950* (New York: Ronald Press Company, 1956), p. 212.

13. Bernard L. Ramm, *The Right, the Good, and the Happy* (Waco, Tex.: Word Books, 1971), p. 85.

14. L. L. McReavy, "The Power of the Church," *Catholics and Divorce*, ed. Patrick J. O'Mahoney (London: Thomas Nelson and Sons, 1959), p. 86.

15. Walter George Smith, "Divorce," *Catholic Encyclopedia*, ed. Charles G. Hermann (New York: The Encyclopedia Press, 1909), V., pp. 62, 63.

16. *Ibid.*, p. 63.

17. McReavy, *op. cit.*, p. 30.

18. W. M. Foley, "Marriage," *Encyclopedia of Religion and Ethics*, ed. James Hastings (New York: Scribner's, 1953), VIII, p. 440.

19. *Ibid.*

20. *Report of the Lambeth Conference 1930, Encyclical Letter from the Bishops with Resolutions and Reports* (New York: Macmillian, 1931), p. 42.

21. *The Lambeth Conference, 1948, The Encyclical Letter from the Bishops together with Resolutions and Reports* (London: S.P.C.K., 1948), p. 100.

22. *Ibid.*

23. *The Lambeth Conference, 1968, Resolutions and Reports* (New York: Seabury Press, 1948), p. 37.

24. Arthur Robert Winnett, *Divorce and Remarriage in Anglicanism (London: Macmillian, 1958), p. 273.*

25. *Ibid.*

26. John R. W. Stott, *Divorce* (Downers Grove, Ill.: InterVarsity Press, 1973), p. 4.

27. *Ibid.*, p. 29

28. *Ibid.*, p. 30.

29. Emerson, *op. cit.*, p. 115.

30. *Ibid.*, p. 112.

31. *Constitution and Canons, The Episcopal Church, 1973* (Seabury Press, 1973), pp. 40, 41.

32. *Luther's Catechism*, with an explanation by Joseph Stump (Philadelphia: The United Lutheran Publication House,1935),pp.65,66.

33. Emerson, *op. cit.*, p. 121.

34. *Ibid.*, pp. 121, 122 (adapted).

35. *Teachings and Practice on Marriage and Divorce* (Minneapolis: Commission on Research and Social Action of the American Lutheran Church, 1965), p. 6.

36. Howard, *op. cit.*, p. 454.

37. *The Constitution of the United Presbyterian Church in the United States, Part I, Book of Confessions* (Philadelphia: The Office of the General Assembly of the United Presbyterian Church in the United States of America, 1967), Article 6.125.

38. *The Constitution of the United Presbyterian Church in the United States of America, Part II, Book of Order, 1976-77* (Philadelphia: The Office of the General Assembly of the United Presbyterian Church in the United States of America, 1967), Article 42.31.

39. *The Book of Discipline of the United Methodist Church, 1972* (Nashville: The United Methodist Publishing House, 1973), Article 350.

40. *Ibid.*

41. Emerson, *op. cit.*, p. 119, taken from *The Discipline of the Methodist Church*, ed. Bishop Nolan M. Harmon (The Methodist Publishing House, 1957), p. 130.

42. *The Book of Discipline of the United Methodist Church 1976* (Nashville: The United Methodist Publishing House, 1976), p. 89.

43. Lawrence G. Wrenn, ed., *Divorce and Remarriage in the Catholic Church* (New York: Newman Press, 1973), especially chapter 3, Prevailing and Countervailing Trends in Non-Catholic Churches."

44. *Ibid.*, pp. 82, 83.

45. *Church of the Nazarene 1952 Manual* (Kansas City, Mo.: Nazarene Publishing House, 1952), p. 47.

46. *Ibid.*, p. 310.

47. *Church of the Nazarene Manual 1976* (Kansas City, Mo.: Nazarene Publishing House, 1976), pp. 47, 48.

48. *Ibid.*, pp. 237, 238.

49. *Manual of The Christian and Missionary Alliance, 1975 Edition* (Nyack, N.Y.: The Christian and Missionary Alliance, 1976), p. 17.

50. *Church of the Brethren Annual Conference, Richmond, Virginia*, Unfinished Business, I. Marriage and Divorce—Appendix: 1964 Report (Elgin, Ill.: Brethren Press, 1977), p. 102.

51. *Ibid.*

52. *Ibid.*

53. *Church of the Brethren Annual Conference, Richmond, Virginia,* Unfinished Business, I. Marriage and Divorce—1977 Report of the Committee (Elgin, Ill.: Brethren Press, 1977), p. 98.

54. J. C. Wenger, ed., *The Complete Writings of Menno Simons,* (Scottdale, Pa.: Herald Press, 1956), p. 200.

55. *Ibid.,* p. 1041.

56. Martin, *op. cit.,* pp. 36, 37.

57. *Ibid.,* p. 38.

58. J. Howard Kauffman and Leland Harder, *Anabaptists Four Centuries Later* (Scottdale, Herald Press, 1975), 174.

59. Ramm, *op. cit.,* p. 89.

CHAPTER III

APPROACHING DIVORCE FROM DIVINE LAW AND FOR-GIVING GRACE

For some persons, being Christian is making sure they endure to the end according to a strict adherence to the "letter of the law." This kind of approach, followed by the Pharisees, provides maximum religious security, at least outwardly, because the exact words of Holy Writ can always be tenaciously held to as the final word on the subject. If these religious folk are asked, "How does that law fit into my situation of a broken marriage and a broken life?" the rationale becomes, "It must apply because that book, chapter, verse, and phrase give the law, and it is up to us to follow and obey it to be happy Christians!

It is therefore helpful for us in this study to understand clearly the concepts of law and grace as they are set forth in both the Old and New Testaments. Need they be paradoxical? If not, wherein does their compatibility lie?

A. Law—Old Testament Concept

The Hebrew word תורה (*torah*) is the basic term used for law in the Old Testament. In Judaism this word is given to the first five books of the Old Testament, the Pentateuch. According to some authorities, its actual meaning is not "law" but "instruction," "guidance," "direction."

> *Torah* is that which points the way for the faithful Israelites and for the community of Israel. Not merely the laws of the Pentateuch provide guidance; the entire story of God's dealings with mankind and with Israel points the way. The term "*Torah*" may therefore stand in the way of an adequate understanding of law in the Old Testament if it is given too prominent a place.[1]

Another scholar says that *Torah* "simply points out the general purpose of the law, viz. that it is for the guidance of God's people in the various matters to which it relates.[2]

The etymology of *Torah* also sheds light in this direction. "*Torah*" is from "*horah*" the Hiphil of "*yarah*." ISBE explains, "The root meaning is to throw; hence in Hiphil the word means to point out (as by throwing out the hand), and so to direct; and "*Torah*" is direction."[3] From this we understand that law in the Old Testament is to be understood as offering human direction. It is important to see "that the end of the law lay beyond the mere obedience to such and such rules, that end being

instruction in the knowledge of God and of man's relation to Him, and guidance in living as the children of
such a God as He revealed Himself to be."[4]

"One writer observes that the arm of the law is "to
bend the people and the individual to Yahweh."[5] The
policies laid down under the body of laws have as their
object the maintenance of life in community. The law
provides the legal understandings of how life in the community is to be lived, and the procedures by which these
policies are closely related to the self-understanding of
Israel as a covenant community under a covenant relationship with God.[6]

These laws and policies apart from a covenant relationship with God lose their spiritual significance. Obviously,
they are still valid for community life. The accounts in
the *Torah* of God dealing with His people—Adam,
Noah, Abraham, Isaac, Jacob, and Joseph—make nice
stories. But one must keep in mind that this revelation is
more than interesting biographies of the patriarchs; it is
God establishing a covenant with His people Israel.
Knight points out that *Torah* means both "teaching" and
"revelation,"[7] and therefore we see in both of these
Yahweh choosing Israel as His people, and Israel acknowledging Yahweh as its God. The *Torah* needs to be
seen as more than a "mere deposit of truth in legal form
meant to be deduced to suit every possible contingency
in human life. [We need to see it] as a growing revelation
of God's ways in the past that acted as a guide for understanding His will for the future, as He led His people by
the Spirit into ever deeper knowledge of what that will
demanded of them."[8]

This extended quote from Kittel's work expresses this
idea well:

The laws are not regarded, then, as a fair adjustment of human interests which is then divinely sanctioned. Nor is their observance the achievement which Israel presents to its God in gratitude for the covenant and election. In particular, it is not the achievement which establishes the divine relationships. The laws are in the strictest sense the requirements of the God to whom Israel belongs because He has revealed Himself in the exodus from Egypt and because in all future wars He will show Himself to be the God of the people. Thus the motive for keeping this law is simply that of obedience insofar as there is any conscious reflection on the questions of motivation.[9]

The law set guidelines for Israel and was intended as well to make an impact on the heathen nations around Israel. Israel was chosen by God to be an instrument that He could use in His plan that *all* nations come to know of His purpose for them. But Knight points out that we have no record that they were impressed to any degree at all. "The reason seems to be a simple one. This legislation probably remained only an ideal."[10] He then points out that it is not difficult to perceive from the prophetic writings that the Hebrew farmer seldom attempted to live up to the high ideals contained in the law. It seems that Israel's influence on her neighbors was weak and had little witness impact. "She possessed a great ideal, enshrined within her Law. But the Law never fully became 'flesh,' and therefore visible to the eyes of men. It remained clauses in a statute book and little more."[11]

Let us look at this in the light of marital laws. In the first chapter we examined God's divine plan as stated in Genesis 2:24: "Therefore a man leaves his father and his mother and cleaves to his wife, and they become one flesh." Marriage was designed to be indissoluble, an enduring relationship through life. We find no provision for divorce and remarriage as a valid part of the order of creation. It was God's original intention and divine principle that marriage be a union for life, i.e., permanent and monogamous. Jesus also confirmed this in Matthew 19:5, 6. Dwight Small observes:

> No divorce or remarriage has been programmed for mankind's marital experience under the conditions of original sinlessness. Only the disruption and disorder of a fallen world could make this a necessary option for mankind. The rupture of this divinely instituted human bond is conceivable only if first of all there is a rupture in the divine-human relation. At the very outset this enunciates the nature and basis of marriage and clearly implies that no dissolution of .the marriage bond could be contemplated except as a radical breach of the divine institution. It was impossible to envision any marital dissolution as anything other than abnormal and evil. Such was the ethical context of "the beginning" when mankind was as yet free from the thralldom of sin.[12]

Later laws in the Old Testament speak to the issue of divorce and remarriage, but nowhere in terms of absolute prohibition. If it were regarded as such, it must be assumed that a divine law of prohibition would have been included in the Mosaic law. It is true that within the body of the Decalogue we have the words, "Thou shalt not commit adultery" (Exodus 20:14). The Pentateuch also speaks to this in Leviticus 18:20 and Deuteronomy 5:18. In Leviticus 20:10 the death penalty was required when this law was broken. However, various concessions were made to this divine ideal. Intercourse with a female slave betrothed to another was not a capital offense—only a guilt offering was needed (Leviticus 19:22).

Along this line, W. J. Harrelson writes:

118

Adultery is categorically prohibited, since it also represents an act in defiance of God. God made mankind male and female; in marriage the two become one (Genesis 1:27; 2:18, 21-24; 1 Corinthians 6:15-17). The act of adultery constitutes a denial of the unity affirmed by Yahweh and is not understood to be compromised by occasional polygamous marriages.[13]

In the Deuteronomy 24:1-4 case, as we have seen, provisions for divorce were given, and therefore allowance for the breaking of the marital union, and hence adultery. The other two instances in Deuteronomy that deal with prohibitions regarding divorce are Deuteronomy 21:10-14 and 22:13-19. The restrictions bring into check a man's liberty to divorce his wife at will. Before these laws, apparently the husband was under no restriction and could divorce his wife on his own initiative whenever he pleased.

It is quite obvious that these laws point out a condition in Israel that was not healthy, and yet no further Mosaic law was laid down in respect to a general rule against divorce. "It is certainly conceded to be status quo, and there is no civil or ecclesiastical ostracism attached to it. On the contrary (in the case of Deuteronomy 24:1-4) it is legal and fully effective in giving the wife the right of remarriage."[14]

Possibly this concession by Moses to allow divorce was for the prevention of even worse situations. In such a case it would be better to tolerate divorce, of which God disapproved, than to produce greater evils through an enforcement of the marriage law. Lovett says, "Thus the divorce machinery was a toleration of man's inability to meet the divine requirement and at the same time a means of preserving justice."[15]

B. Law—New Testament Concept

By "law" (νόμος —nomos) or "the law" (ὁ νόμος —o nomos) as used in the New Testament, what is generally referred to is the law of God as revealed in the Old Testament. And at first glance it would seem that Jesus was ambivalent toward the value of the law for those who would fear God in His time. First of all, we see in Christ what might be called a criticism of the law. Various facets of Christ's words and ministry in the Synoptics emphasized that the law, as understood by Judaism, no longer regulated the ways of God with men, and that Jesus Himself had taken over the place previously held by the law. "The law and the prophets were until John; since then the good news of the kingdom of God is preached" (Luke 16:16; cf. Matthew 11:11-13). A new order came through Christ. How is this seen?

Christ's parables pointed out that the kingdom of God is now in the process of realizing itself. Jesus became a friend of sinners, therefore ignoring limitations placed on social intercourse by the law. When we examine some of Mark's writings, we find Jesus taking a controversial stance on what should or should not be done on the Sabbath (Mark 2:23—3:6). A large portion of Mark 7 (verses 1-24) deals with things clean and unclean—a position quite startling to the Pharisees, the strict keepers of the ceremonial laws. And we also observe Christ's attitude toward divorce. He abrogates the looseness of the traditional laws regarding divorce proceedings and reaches back to God's original intent in marriage in Genesis. However, Christ was not bringing back a restricting marriage law, but was communicating that marriage is ideally a self-giving, loving relationship between male and female. It is not an empty legal contract. Through these so-called criticisms of the law, Christ was elevating moral law above ceremonial laws and was rejecting oral tradition.

The whole gospel message points out the emptiness and inadequacy of a strict adherence to the law, but instead Christ challenged men and women, with humble readiness, to receive God's grace.

Jesus pointed out that total obedience to the will of God (an obedience based on love) could not be reduced to a written code. If a person obeys God, he has the freedom, according to Christ, to discover how obedience can best be expressed, as long as he keeps in proper focus the law, tradition, and the words of Jesus Himself. Christ knew that if one follows the law with all its demands, it would only lead to a preoccupation with reward and merit if love is absent, and in the end would produce a great specimen of a hypocrite.

> (Christ) himself spoke, not primarily at least, as a law-giver, though he commanded, but as one sent of God in the last hour to reveal the absolute will of God. His hyperbolical statements of the demand of God, though to be taken with the utmost seriousness, are, therefore, to be interpreted, not as a new law, but as pointers to the true nature of God's demand of love.[16]

And, taking the whole New Testament into consideration, we note that these documents

> find in the law both the passing shadow of the gospel to come and that which is completed or fulfilled "in Christ." They all affirm that the law, insofar as it is the expression of the holy will of God, remains valid, radicalized, and at the same time relativized by the absolute claim of love.[17]

Manson points out the following:

It is a mistake to regard the ethical teaching of Jesus as a "New Law" in the sense of a reformed and simplified exposition of the Old, or as a code of rules to take the place of the code of Moses and his successors. What Jesus offers in His ethical teaching is not a set of rules of conduct, but a number of illustrations of the way in which a transformed character will express itself in conduct.[18]

Dare the church today, then, reinstitute itself as a legal body when it comes to the question of broken marital relations among its own people? It is the church's mission, instead, to inspire persons to espouse a transformed life first. Then ethical demands will follow. However, these demands will find root in the inner consciousness, and not from a manual of discipline. The ethical code of the New Testament will give instruction, direction, and guidance, as did the *Torah*. However, at no time will God's love for the individual be short-circuited in the event the ethical code is broken. Neither is it God's will that the church become a judicial body or a penal institution meting out justice against those persons who have not lived up to the ethical ideal in a perfect manner. Instead it is called to be a conveyor of God's forgiving love even in the midst of a marriage that is on the rocks, or one that ends in divorce.

C. Grace—Old Testament Concept

Let us turn now from the concept of law to the concept of grace as found in the Old and New Testaments. Two Hebrew words, especially, carry the concept of grace in the Old Testament. The verb חנן (*chanan*) occurs 56 times and expresses the turning of one person to another as in an act of assistance. Kittel says, "But חנן (*chanan*) does not just denote the kind disposition and then the outer act as something detached from the inner mood. It rather means the attitude of a person in its direction to another in a specific gracious action."[19] In 41 of the 56 occurrences of the basic stem in the Old Testament, Yahweh is the subject of grace. In the Psalms, for instance, God is called upon many times in prayers of complaint, i.e., to hear the prayers, to heal, to pardon sins, and the like.

However, scholars point out that חסד (*chesed*) is closer to the New Testament χάρις (*charis*) than חנן (*chanan*). It means a "loyal devotion grounded in love which goes beyond legal obligation and can be depended on to the utmost."[20] Kittel defines it as kindliness or friendliness.[21] It is translated in the RSV as "steadfast love."

The word חסד (*chesed*) is a particularly suitable word to denote what takes place in the covenant between Yahweh and Israel. For example, Deuteronomy 7:9 (RSV) says, "Know therefore that the Lord your God is God, the faithful God who keeps covenant and steadfast love with those who love him and keep his commandments, to a thousand generations." Kittel says, "The use of חסד עשה (*chesed asah*) makes it plain that this is . . . a reference to grace converted into act." In the phrase, "to a thousand generations," חסד (*chesed*) is maintained as incomparably stronger than the burning wrath of the jealous God. Hence חסד (*chesed*) occurs elsewhere in Yahweh predications whether they contain a reference to the One who visits sin or are limited on the other hand to salvation formulations.[22]

It is interesting to follow God's attribute of grace as it appears in specific acts in the Old Testament. In Exodus 22:27 God is gracious in hearing prayer and in Exodus

32:12 He is gracious in departing from His anger. Even in the midst of the Fall, Adam and Eve are not left standing with condemnation hanging over them, but are given a ray of hope in God's promise in Genesis 3:15 and are shown mercy for their physical well-being by His giving them clothing in 3:21. Later on, Noah is offered special grace, and Abraham is selected to be the forerunner of the new revelation. Israel, then, is chosen to be a nation set apart by God's special grace.

Throughout Israel's history from the wilderness wanderings through the time of the Judges, and into the Period of Captivity, God's patience and mercy endured. In the midst of continual apostasy, God's arm reached out to a destitute people.

There were instances where even in His anger God showed mercy. As He was lamenting over the destruction and conflagration that came upon Judah, Jeremiah made statements such as these in Lamentations 3:22-33 (RSV), "The steadfast love of the Lord never ceases. . . . The Lord is good to those who wait for him. . . . For the Lord will not cast off for ever, but, though he cause grief, he will have compassion . . . for he does not willingly afflict or grieve the sons of men."

It is striking that even though in the Old Testament the concept of God's "steadfast love" is normally directed toward God's chosen people who are closely knit to Him in a covenant relationship, there are instances where חסד (*chesed*) is used to describe God's grace reaching out to sinful and undeserving people. For example, God promised to David that His חסד (*chesed*) will not depart from his offspring, even if they "commit iniquity" (2 Samuel 7:14, 15); and in Isaiah 54:8 God's חסד (*chesed*) is offered to disobedient people. These rare exceptions do indicate a certain anticipation of the New Testament teaching.[23] God's gracious purpose was extended to those who were not of Israel and embraced them also. It reached out to those heathen who were brought through Israel into the enjoyment of some of Israel's privileges.

In the Old Testament, grace was mediated to the individual through the nation. We read historical accounts of certain individuals who were forgiven because they were members of a chosen people. They were elect because the nation was set apart by God. Grace, at this point, did not encompass the dimensions of New Testament grace; yet it was present. Steward points out in her article on grace:

> If thus in the view of the Psalmists and the Prophets there is no limit to God's willingness to be reconciled, if even His judgment has a core of mercy, and His love always proves itself stronger than human sin, the other side of Old Testament religion is, in turn, not to be minimized. . . . This covenant takes the form of law. The people are bound to obedience, and the blessings of the covenant can be enjoyed only on this condition. So far from grace being ignored in the Old Testament, it permeates it . . . throughout. But grace is not yet fully revealed; it is still dominated by the ideas of righteousness and retribution. . . . Thus, though by no means the sole element, law remains the distinctive element. . . . In the Old Testament [God's] anger against sin is declared, [but] his mercy and longsuffering are proclaimed; but these rest side by side, an unsolved antimony, waiting the fuller revelation.[24]

D. Grace—New Testament Concept

In the English New Testament the word "grace" is always a translation of χάρις (*charis*), a word that occurs over 170 times in the Greek text. It is not necessary in this study to attempt to deal adequately with the many meanings χάρις (*charis*) has which evolved through secular Greek into biblical usage, but primarily it seems to denote pleasant external appearance such as "gracefulness" and "loveliness" do.[25]

Bullinger's lexicon and concordance describes χάρις (*charis*) as "a kind, affectionate, pleasing nature and inclining disposition, either in a person or thing."[26] For the purposes of our study, the subjective quality the word possesses refers to an inclining towards, a courteous disposition, a friendly willingness. Bullinger goes on to explain χάρις (*charis*) as it especially relates to our study:

> The word denotes, specially, God's grace and favor manifested towards mankind or to any individual which, as a free act, is no more hindered by sin than it is conditioned upon works. It is the grace of God because it denotes the relation assumed and maintained by God towards sinful man. It is joined with Christ, because it is manifested in and through Him.[27]

The predominate usage of χάρις (*charis*) in the New Testament refers to God's favor or undeserved kindness. It is this idea that the Apostle Paul sets forth in his epistles. And the concept that this word holds is not an inactive kind of favor. Burton Easton writes, "A favorable 'thought' of God's about a man involves of necessity the reception of some blessing by that man, and 'to look with favor' is one of the commonest Biblical paraphrases for 'bestowing a blessing,' "[28] In human terms we may refer to a father looking with favor on his children. But this could be taken to mean that he passively sits by and smiles with appreciation concerning what his children are doing. But not so with God. Instead, there exists active power.

For instance, Paul says in 1 Corinthians 15:10, "Not I, but the grace of God which was with me" labored more abundantly than they all. Here grace is something that labors.

It is important also that we look beyond the actual usage of the word to consider the divine activity that mirrors this grace. For instance, in the Gospels the word "grace" hardly appears at all according to Paul's usage of it, but yet we see God's gracious dealings with His children woven into the fabric of the Gospels. God's grace can be seen in its fullness by the divine involvement in human affairs. The whole ministry of Jesus is an act of grace. The Gospels highlight Christ's loving concern for the outcasts of society. He became known as a friend of sinners.

In one story after another Christ sets forth God's generosity. The prodigal son (Luke 15:11-24), the heartbroken tax collector (Luke 18:14), and the parable of the workers in the vineyard (Matthew 20:1-15) all teach the magnanimity of God toward man. As Mitton puts it, "God's dealings with men . . . are not based on a niggardly calculation of what each one deserves, but handed out in almost reckless extravangance, 'good measure, pressed down, shaken together, running over' (Luke 6:38)."[29]

The climactic act of grace was God unselfishly giving Himself in the form of His only Son, Jesus Christ. The death of Jesus, as with the incarnation act, presses home the fact that the Word came to us "full of grace and truth."

E. A Summary

In summarizing the concepts of law and grace that run through both the Old and New Testaments, let us now apply them to our study of divorce and remarriage.

Within our exegetical study we discovered some clear teachings regarding God's divine ideal for marriage. But we also encountered a smattering of cases where the divine ideal was not fulfilled by men and women and we saw their resultant consequences. God has been flexible and long-suffering in His dealings with sinful man. In Matthew 5:32 and 19:9 "except for fornication," is allowed despite the original intent of "cleave unto his wife" in Genesis 2:24. In 1 Corinthians 7:15, "A brother or a sister is not under bondage in such cases" is permitted while "let not man put asunder" in Matthew 19:6 recedes into the background. Although adaptations and accommodations were made, we can in no way perceive these as negating God's intention or His absolute will.

The laws and rules set forth by God in the whole of Scripture are taken to reflect the intention of God. Theologically, we finite creatures have no right or even reason to doubt this. This is God's righteous standard. However, "a grave necessity, an impossible situation imposed by human failure is then a matter of God's grace and the accommodation of His conditional will."[30] Or said in another way, "The absolute (which I interpret as meaning law) gives form to God's pure and original intent—His absolute, uncompromised righteousness. Grace gives form to God's present enactment of His conditional will on behalf of human weakness and failure, to accommodate His will to weakness and need."[31]

Dwight Small comments regarding God's intent to meet man on his level, and yet invite him higher:

Grace, then, conditions God's will by providing full and free forgiveness, by renewing life's possibilities on the basis of Christ's atoning work. The conditional will of God expresses His expectation that redeemed men and women cannot, under the conditions of this age, reach perfect righteousness. Man's response to God's absolute will shall always be relative, a partial fulfillment at best. The redeemed person stands continually within the forgiving grace of God in Christ. This is what it means to be 'in Christ.' Not that there is no expectation of major fulfillment of God's will; on the contrary, every provision has been made for Christian life to appropriate God's resources for spiritual and moral growth!

Somewhat paradoxically, then, we speak of God's absolute unconditional will for man while at the same time we speak of His conditional will. . . . One time it is *law;* another *grace.* Under law, God acts graciously; under *grace,* God points to the law as the standard of His righteousness and as the goal of life in the Spirit. The different modes of administering His will correlate with the different provisions for man's enablement. Under Mosaic Law, God's people were left to the strength of their own desires and will. During the Church Age, a higher, more internal standard is placed before the redeemed. It demands an inward conformity to God's will rather than a response to law. But with the higher standard there is also provided the indwelling of the Holy Spirit; He is the dynamic power given for the fulfillment of God's will.[32]

Let us look at an example that may assist us in our understanding of this seeming dualism. What did Jesus do when thrust in the midst of a situation where there was a case of proven adultery? The Pharisees wondered how Jesus would respond to their challenge of keeping the law as set forth in the Mosaic code. The story is told in John 8:3-11.[33] Verse 6 clearly states, "This they said to test him, that they might have some charge to bring against him" (RSV). In this instance Jesus moved their thinking in a direction which actually seemed to oppose the harsh penalty of the Mosaic law. Jesus was not disregarding the seriousness of the act. His law is absolute and uncompromised. But when He said, "Let him who is without sin among you be the first to throw a stone at her," He put grace above law. A life was broken. A soul was crushed. He turned to the woman and said, "Neither do I condemn you; go, and do not sin again."

Jesus, being God, gave the law. Now He *does* something different from what He *says*. What a striking contrast! But it is not a contradiction. It only points out the nature of grace as it is applied by the Author of the law. This example, possibly more than anything else, introduces to us the transition Jesus was making from law to the grace which was to rule in the age of the church.

The church today is caught in the bind of upholding the law's ideal without compromising, and yet being sensitive to human need. My intent in this chapter has been to point out that a contradiction does not exist between the old and new covenants that God brought to man. It was necessary to build a basis of law in the Old Testament so that grace could be seen in its proper dimensions in the New Testament. It is my firm conviction that the revelatory process in the Old Testament led to a fuller revelation in the New Testament. Through the process of unfolding revelation, with God speaking and man responding, God's grace was made more evident. The New Testament is built upon the Old Testament, with Christ and His redemptive work being the epitome of God's acts in the biblical narrative. But even so we have seen that throughout the Old Testament God's redemptive acts and abundant grace were made evident to many persons in various kinds of situations.

It is not necessary to choose between the Old Testament law and New Testament grace—one or the other. They are not mutually exclusive or antithetical. However, quoting chapters and verses can bring a Christian under bondage to the law. A pastor must decide whether he will preach that life must be controlled by chapters and verses or whether he encourages that life be regulated according to divine operating principles. The divine operating principles grow out of law and are superior to it.

A divorced person once confided to me, "I feel God is a realist." I hear this person saying that God has enacted the laws, but He also meets us and accepts us where we are. Biblical law allows for God's forgiveness, but we must appropriate that mercy and grace. God's forgiveness releases the spiritual or psychological forgiveness of ourselves. It is a combination of God's law and grace that move us ahead in Him.

Notes: Chapter III

1. W. J. Harrelson, "Law" *The Interpreters Dictionary of the Bible*, Ed. George Arthur Buttrick (New York: Abingdon Press, 1962), III, p. 77.

2. Ulric Z. Rule, "Law in the Old Testament," *The International Standard Biblical Encyclopedia*, ed. James Orr (Chicago: The Howard Severance Company, 1925), III, p. 1852.

3. *Ibid.*

4. *Ibid.*

5. Kleinknecht, Gutbrod, *Nomos* in G. Kittel, Gerhard Friedrich, ed. *Theological Dictionary of the New Testament* trans. and ed. by Geoffrey W. Bromily (Grand Rapids, Mich.: William B. Eerdmans Publishing Company, 1967), IV, p. 1037.

6. Harrelson, *op. cit.*, p. 77.

7. George A. F. Knight, *Law and Grace* (Philadelphia: Westminster Press, 1962), p. 53.

8. *Ibid.*, p. 54.

9. Kleinknecht, Gutbrod, *op. cit.*, p. 1036.

10. Knight, *op. cit.*, p. 34.

11. *Ibid.*

12. Dwight Hervey Small, *The Right to Remarry* (Old Tappen, N.J.: Revell, 1975), p. 32.

13. W. J. Harrelson, "Marriage," *The Interpreters Dictionary of the Bible*, ed. George Arthur Buttrick (New York: Abingdon Press, 1962), IV, p. 571.

14. Small, *op. cit.*, p. 38.

15. C. S. Lovett, *The Compassionate Side of Divorce* (Baldwin Park, Calif.: Personal Christianity, 1975) pp. 34, 35.

16. W. D. Davis, "Law in the New Testament" *The Interpreters Dictionary of the Bible*, ed. George Arthur Buttrick (New York: Abingdon Press, 1962), III, pp. 97, 98.

17. *Ibid.*, p. 102.

18. T. W. Manson, *The Teachings of Jesus* (Cambridge: Cambridge University Press, 1935), p. 301.

19. Conzelmann, Zimmerli, *Charis* in G. Kittel, Gerhard Friedrich ed., *Theological Dictionary of the New Testament*, trans. and ed. by Geoffrey W. Bromiley (Grand Rapids, Mich.: Eerdman's, 1974), IX, p. 377.

20. C. L. Mitton, "Grace" *The Interpreters Dictionary of the Bible*, ed. George Arthur Buttrick (New York: Abingdon Press, 1962), II, p. 467.

21. Conzelmann, Zimmerli, *op. cit.*, p. 381.

22. *Ibid.*, p. 383.

23. Mitton, *op. cit.*, p. 468.

24. Grace A. Steward, "Grace" *A Dictionary of the Bible*, ed. James Hastings (New York: Scribner's, 1899), p. 255.

25. Burton Scott Easton, "Grace" *The International Biblical Encyclopaedia*, ed. James Orr (Chicago: Howard-Severance Company, 1925), II, p. 1290.

26. Ethelbert W. Bullinger, "Grace" *A Critical Lexicon and Concordance to the English and Greek New Testament* (Grand Rapids, Mich.: Zondervan Publishing House, 1975), p. 341.

27. *Ibid.*

28. Easton, *op. cit.*, p. 1290.

29. Mitton, *op. cit.*

30. Small, *op. cit.*, p. 175.

31. *Ibid.*, p. 25.

32. *Ibid.*, pp. 133, 134.

33. This passage is not found in the earliest New Testament manuscripts, and appears in the RSV as a footnote.

CHAPTER IV

THE CHURCH AS AN EXPRESSION OF FORGIVENESS IN RELATION TO DIVORCED PERSONS

A. The Church Teaches Mercy and Forgiveness of God

"How does it feel to be 'just separated' "? Jane Lamb writes. "Take a look at me. . . . Color me a wreck. . . . My world was gone—everything I had believed in, everything I pinned my hopes on. I had once been loved, but was no longer"[1]

Along with her all-alone syndrome, Jane felt that she had no identity. She just didn't fit anywhere. She knew that hurt persons need a good environment in which to heal. They need a place where they can feel accepted no matter what their emotional state or life situation. On other occasions she always had found this at church. But she writes:

> After separation, church just was not the same. I tried go-
> ing to church but I would come home crying every time. . . .
> I cannot begin to tell you how it felt to need God so badly,
> yet feel unacceptable. I tried talking to a minister about my
> feelings, but his only question was, "Did you have a scrip-
> tural reason for divorcing?" After that I quit going.[2]

Last year over one million couples were divorced in
the United States and Canada. They are becoming a fast-
growing minority in our society. In its position and in its
teaching, where will the church stand? There are three
alternatives it can take in relation to the divorced. The
first position is one of hostility and standoffishness, a bar-
rier which denominational tradition and personal preju-
dice has set up. This keeps out all persons who may be
problems for theology and local congregational cultural
accretions. Some denominations in general polity and
practice have withdrawn from getting involved in this
kind of social ill. Some religious groups have tended to
keep aloof from outside social and cultural trends. Their
ingrownness and isolation many times forced families to
stay together. Divorce, to them, was no alternative.
However, even in these groups the social structure is
changing, and they are confronted now with the decision
of continuing in their aloof stance and turning personal
need away, or, with a sensitive heart, giving compassionate attention to these needs.

A second position is one of welcoming such persons
into the fellowship and sharing with them the idea that
it's okay to have them around. This stance is one of
tolerance. This position would say, "We don't feel right
in sending you away because the church is here to accept
all persons, and so we hope you can fit into our program
all right." The onus is placed on them. They need to

work hard to try to measure up. If they can survive long enough, after a period of time they will feel integrated—hopefully.

A third alternative is one of deliberate acceptance, assimilation, and ministry to divorced persons. In this case, the divorced or remarried person is not from the start looked upon as a second-class citizen or held in social punishment in order to teach him/her a lesson. The forgiveness of God is taught and shown to this person. If he/she shows repentance for past sin and commits his/her life to discipleship, membership is made valid and meaningful. This therapeutic approach accepts persons as they are, and on the basis of their relationship with God, they become integrated completely into the life of the congregation.

Many churches tend toward one of the first two alternatives. But how can such a church fulfill its mission in teaching God's forgiveness and mercy? The responsibility, in the main, lies with the pastor. He needs to act as a counselor to instill in his members that God is not only a sovereign, holy God who reenacts Mt. Sinai dramas causing persons to be fearful and trembling. He is also the God of Mt. Calvary who bids all men, "Come just as you are."

Teaching is needed regarding the duty of fully forgiving and warmly receiving into fellowship all penitent sinners who come to Christ with their load of sin and guilt. The pastor must challenge his people that today, in this complex twentieth century, we have a Christ who is the full answer to the needs of men and women regardless of how they lived in the past. Throughout Jesus' ministry it seems obvious that He was "more interested in the healing of broken relationships than in producing good people. Hence, Jesus introduced Himself as Savior and Healer."[3] As Savior and Healer, and not only Revealer, Jesus brought to us a gospel that is adequate for all kinds of human predicaments—even those which involve such situations as divorce and remarriage.

Is the church today able to mediate this kind of revelation to persons steeped in guilt and despair? Too often Christians, intent on being seriously committed to New Testament truth, have passed judgment on the divorced rather than extend God's grace and forgiveness. Quoting chapter, verse, and phrase, often out of context, only causes further heartache and does not fulfill the commission of the divine Counselor and Healer.

One divorcee shares his feeling of rejection:

> The hardest reactions came from persons who wanted to be [my] friends but for whom divorce was not an option. . . . The theological position was more important than the brokenness of the person sitting in his livingroom. If that's gospel, then it's not spelled "good news." It is this very feeling of nonconformity, nonacceptance, which continues the alienation process for the already painfully separated person. In my experience it has been the church's previous position of emphasizing the failure related to divorce which has perpetuated this treatment of persons.[4]

Bernard Ramm speaks for solving "some of these wretchedly complex cases by a spirit of love, of understanding, and of redemption. . . . The attempt is to salvage or redeem life rather than to treat people in a strict, moralistic, and legalistic manner."[5]

It is true that the pastor and church leaders must teach that permanent marriage is God's divine intent. But these leaders, along with the laity must face the discrepancy between the ideal as seen in Scripture and the practical application in the everyday Christian walk.

Poettcker points out:

> As with many areas, be they race, or alcoholism . . . so also with marriage, the church is constantly called upon to face the question of how far she must adjust her action to the failures of sinful men to attain the divine intention. Every time we say that we need to get back to the principles of the Early Church, we are acknowledging that we have adjusted through past failures, or that we have slipped from the higher ideal.[6]

This quote may help us to see that God's forgiveness is present even in the situations described above. The pastor must in his teaching and preaching not give the impression that he is accepting whatever law (or lack of law) is convenient. The church can accept no law but the law of Christ, nor dare she ever be found witnessing to anything less than the highest divine intention for mankind in every area of life. And yet, while carrying forth this witness, the church must deal with the human situation here and now. This means sympathizing and dealing realistically with those who have been overtaken in faults and caught in the depths of despair because of their sinfulness.

It is difficult at times to sense the magnanimity of God's forgiveness. Some persons have applied it to certain sins and not others, or have said it will go so far and no farther. No doubt this misconception is based many times on one's own psychological power (or lack of power) to forgive.

One congregation, after making a careful study of divorce and remarriage and the forgiveness of God, listed verses for application and diagrammed its results as follows:

Forgiveness:

Matthew 18:15-20   Model for dealing with offender within the church.

John 8:3-11   Jesus forgives a woman taken in adultery.

Matthew 6:12, 14, 15   (Lord's Prayer.) Man determines the extent of God's forgiveness.

Colossians 3:13   "Forgiving each other, as the Lord has forgiven you, so you also must forgive" (Ephesians 4:32).

2 Corinthians 5:17   The forgiven sinner is a new creation in Christ.

2 Corinthians 5:18-20   Being reconciled with God, the Christian now becomes an agent of reconciliation.

Here's an illustration of God's vs. man's forgiveness:

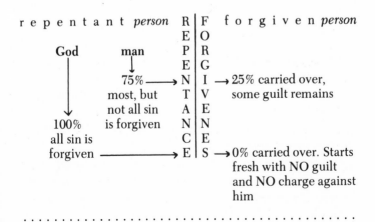

```
r e p e n t a n t  person   R | F    f o r g i v e n  person
                            E | O
     God         man        P | R
                     ↓      E | G
               75% ———→ N | I → 25% carried over,
               most, but    T | V      some guilt remains
               not all sin  A | E
      100%     is forgiven  N | N
      all sin is            C | E
      forgiven ————————→ E | S → 0% carried over. Starts
                                       fresh with NO guilt
                                       and NO charge against
                                       him
```

OR, see it this way: in the kingdom to come (eternity) the repentant sinner will be forgiven, but now (1978) not all sin can be forgiven, consequently church membership must be denied.

Repentant Person

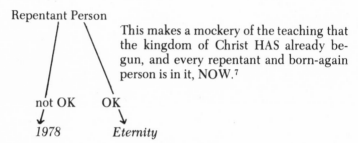

This makes a mockery of the teaching that the kingdom of Christ HAS already begun, and every repentant and born-again person is in it, NOW.[7]

not OK   OK

1978   *Eternity*

In divorce situations when persons in the church offer a spate of words about rules that dare not be broken, the pastor needs to answer with the rules of redemption.

By offering forgiveness to persons broken by sin, we are contributing to wholeness. Abraham Schmitt says:

> Whenever people are involved in helping to return to the unity that existed before the fall of man, then they are nearest the center of God's will. To hate is to sever relationship; thus it is the greatest sin. To love is to bind the brokenness of sin; thus it is the greatest commandment.[8]

When we can be charitable and redemptive to persons who have not lived up to the unity before the Fall, we are fulfilling God's command. Pastoral leadership can move to the forefront of showing grace, following in the steps of Jesus who demonstrated more affirmation than condemnation, especially for those who are already feeling guilty. If this can be illustrated by pastors, teaching will occur. What is taught may not be really so important as what is caught. And congregational members who take upon them the challenge of grace for those in need will, in turn, experience within their congregation a new outpouring of grace from God. The prayer traditionally known as the Lord's Prayer will reach fulfillment in the part that says, "Forgive us our debts as we forgive our debtors."

Possibly one of the reasons congregational members cannot seem to forgive is that they have not come to grips with the question of who was really responsible for the marital relationships that ended in divorce. Wayne Oates suggests that the church community is a corporate body. We, therefore, share responsibility for each other's attitudes, actions, failures, and successes.

> The hardness of the church in its care of the divorcees is a tacit confession of the guilt of the church for its timidity, its negligence, and its lack of discipline in attending the spiritual needs of the couple before marriage, shortly after marriage, and during the period of separation. . . . We should not reduce the weight of sin, condemnation, and guilt attached to divorce. Rather, we should distribute it and accept our fair share of it.[9]

On the same point, Abraham Schmitt writes:

> In the final analysis, we are all a partner in the cause—if not by commission, then by omission. We are a part of a society that perpetuates divorce and thus a part of each faltering piece. So how can we cast a stone?[10]

It is imperative that counseling services be provided to persons considering marriage to help them understand the seriousness and responsibilities of marriage. Opportunities should be offered so that couples can talk over problems with church leaders and church members.

If adequate services are available, there may be more congregational acceptance of a dead-end marriage in that members will not feel loaded down by guilt because of inadequate interest beforehand.

We have seen, then, that God's redemptive grace is extended in all kinds of human situations. Forgiveness is available. But sometimes that forgiveness is not mediated through the congregation to the one standing in need which causes the divorcee to feel even more guilt.

Part of my data gathering for this study included sending questionnaires to pastors and divorced persons. One question I asked divorced persons was, "Have you felt forgiven by your congregation?" One lady wrote, "I don't know—my main forgiveness had to come from God. Although I had been remarried for ten years, it was only last year that my minister helped me work out my guilt feelings."

In a personal interview with one divorcee, I posed the question, "Did you feel that your sense of rejection brought about more guilt feelings?"

"Very much so," was the reply. "Discrimination seemed to bring about a sense of lasting guilt feelings."

And yet even if God forgives, and the person senses forgiveness from the group, the process of forgiveness may still be quenched unless the person forgives himself.

James G. Emerson calls this "realized forgiveness." It refers specifically to a personal experience, not only a doctrinal issue. It is the awareness of forgiveness to such a degree that a person is free from the guilt he feels. For this to happen, he must have a knowledge of his genuine guilt. "The experience of realized forgiveness is the positive dimension that makes one free from bondage to a past guilt."[11]

The foregoing thoughts actually lay the base for further congregational involvement with divorced persons. If the church cannot first overcome its own guilt—if the minister feels guilty about taking a redemptive approach toward a situation because he is not sure of the scriptural principles or the church's stand—how can either of these hope to mediate forgiveness to the couple? Both pastor and congregation can be so bound by a sense of guilt which results in vacillation and confusion that they are not free to minister to the needs crying out from the depths of brokenness.

B. The Church Perceives the Human Predicament in the Midst of Our Society's Complexities

In *Future Shock,* Alvin Toffler envisions shifts of family life in our changing society that will destroy our traditional concept of marriage. And some of these have already arrived on the scene. Temporary marriages, trial marriages, and serial marriages are becoming a pattern rather than an exception in modern life. Says Professor Jessie Bernard, a prominent family sociologist: "Plural marriage is more extensive in our society today than it is in societies that permit polygamy—the chief difference being that we have institutionalized plural marriages serially or sequentially rather than contemporaneously."[12]

In fifteen years the divorce rate has almost tripled. In 1961 there were 414,000 divorces in the United States and in 1976 there were almost 1,100,000.

How does the church respond to this? Wes Bryan writes,

Often the church's approach to divorce is: if you preach hard enough, loud enough, and long enough, "divorce" will go away. Well, it hasn't gone away. Instead, those staggering statistics compel us to put down last year's sermon notes with all the proof texts and look through our own restless marriages to individual lives.[13]

It is important that the church attempt to understand the forces that give birth to marital disruptions. Possibly this will evoke more understanding among churches today.

R. Lofton Hudson summarizes a section in his book by saying that most really bad marriages are those which:

(1) Were simply bad choices in the first place—some people are so incompatible that they cannot stand each other.

(2) Two people slide into some kind of faulty and pathological relationship so that their staying together becomes untenable.

(3) The cost of preserving the marriage becomes too high for one or both.

(4) One, because of inner reasons, perhaps mental illness, even physical disability or unwillingness to live in the depriving situation, decides to leave the marriage.

(5) Both feel that they do not find enough rewards in the marriage and therefore mutually agree to call it quits.[14]

As two lovers repeat their marital vows to one another at the altar surrounded by all the loveliness of a beautiful church ceremony, the prospect of insurmountable marriage problems is scarcely conceivable. All is well. Happiness certainly lies ahead. And yet for some there are minor nagging doubts. In one instance, a bride questioned whether she was taking the right step as she proceeded down the aisle. And this marriage a few years later ended in divorce. But, on the whole, two people generally enter the marriage relationship with the highest ideals and expectations.

At this point in their lives, the young couple is not aware of the ruthless wedges of environment in the complex human situation of twentieth-century urban life that will be pressuring them apart. The old adage applies here—"Things are not the same as they used to be!" The media, especially television, bombard the home every day of the year with a value system different from that which the church attempts to practice. Today, from childhood, a person is exposed to casual mores of society concerning marriage. A Catholic writer, Victor J. Pospishil, points out that "the media may not propagate divorce directly, but only show it as appropriate and normal in various marital situations."[15] Anyone vaguely aware of television's afternoon soap operas knows that in most every story sequential cheating on one's spouse—illicit affairs, separations, divorces, and remarriages—are the standard plots which keep the stories alive. These are the ingredients that cause millions of viewers to neglect their afternoon work and become soap opera addicts!

But not only does a person watch marital breakups among fictitious characters. Mass media also makes one aware of the frequency of divorce and remarriage among the prominent people of his country, people who in other respects call forth one's admiration. And even more influential are close friends' parents, schoolteachers, or fellow employees who pronounce a moratorium on their marriage.

Beyond the actual exposure to divorce, married couples are assailed by many other environmental forces that come to them from their social milieu. Many of these stresses cause individuals to head toward the divorce courts. They include dope addiction, homosexuality, and various sorts of mental illness, along with alcoholism and brutality. Extramarital affairs are common today and persons overshadowed by the umbrella of the church are no exception. Uncontrollable tempers and extreme selfishness are as old as time, and yet these are urged on us by technology which offers modern consumers immediate satisfaction.

When negative factors such as these continue in a marriage over the years, they often kill the love one has for the other. Soon, an internal divorce takes place. Then legal divorce simply becomes the outward manifestation of the inward division. But dare we say that any of these are causes that produce irreconcilable differences that inevitably lead to a legal divorce? On the contrary, Lovett suggests that before a Christian considers divorce he should ask himself three questions:

(1) Has our marriage really been dissolved at the heart level?

(2) Is it within my power to effect a spiritual reunion through a deeper commitment to the Lord and a change in my behavior?

(3) Am I willing to give the Lord a chance to do what He can through me to make sure the separation is not of my own doing?[16]

It must be strongly emphasized that a Christian cannot escape from his own moral responsibility to his marriage by excusing himself as part of our modern society. But the point needs to be made to the church today that Christ is also the Christ of culture. The church need not retreat to the hinterlands of the unknown in order to escape temptation to sin. Christ adapts Himself to our culture and our need. He walks among us in a culture whose devious forces move us like pawns for the kill on a chessboard. Niebuhr says:

> Christ belongs in culture because culture itself, without "sense and taste for the infinite," without a "holy music" accompanying all its work, becomes sterile and corrupt. This Christ of religion does not call upon men to leave homes and kindred for His sake; He enters into their homes and all their associations as the gracious presence which adds an aura of infinite meaning to all temporal tasks. [17]

Christ does not cease to get involved in the dirty complexities of divorce even though factors surrounding twentieth-century divorce are different from those of the first century. He works through individuals, pastors, ethicists, and scriptural interpreters to make sure His will and the genuine happiness of the persons involved are fulfilled. It is left to us today to apply biblical principles to the problems that realistically enter into the ethics of marriage and divorce. Unfortunately the New Testament does not contain exhaustive ethics for this purpose. But one thing is clear from Scripture—living under grace is not easy. Christ is our contemporary, as Kierkegaard calls Him, so that He can figure out with us the answers to complex questions. The Bible is not a rule book—New Testament Christianity is not a moralistic religion. The Bible is not a computer to which you can pose a problem and immediately receive a solution. A person weighed down with serious marital difficulties finds himself/ herself searching for direction. And if he is really intent on living out his Christian commitment in the marital maze, he needs to search hard for a resolution. Giving up, or simply pleading the "exception clause," and not striving with all that lies within him to put things back together is less than Christian. Lovett says:

> For believers to forsake their partners merely because they can't get along is no solution. That is defeat. The very concept of Christian victory implies a Christian fight. Until a person has worked hard to be the kind of mate he should be, divorce ought to be out of the question. Those who run because they find it too difficult to live with a certain person, generally find they haven't escaped the problem. The difficulty lies within them, so that no matter how much they run, they take the problem with them.[18]

As mentioned earlier, two young persons come to the marriage altar with the highest ideals. But suppose something unaccountable goes wrong. Suppose what was entered into as one of life's greatest joys becomes hell on earth?

William Barclay writes:

> But if it should happen that two people find living together an impossibility; if they have consulted the doctor and the minister and the psychologist and the psychiatrist; if they have taken all the guidance that there is to take, and if the situation is still beyond mending, then I do not think that it is an act of Christian love to keep two such people tied together in a life that is a torture; nor do I think that it is right for them only to be allowed to separate and never be allowed to try to start again. In such circumstances I believe it is the action of Christian love, for I do not think Jesus would have insisted that two utterly incompatible people should be condemned to drag out a loveless existence, heartbreaking for themselves and disastrous for their children. Nor do I believe that they should be forbidden to remarry and to remarry with the blessing of the church. Nor do I think that I would wish to talk much about innocent and not innocent parties, for when a marriage breaks up I

should doubt if there is any such thing as an altogether innocent and an altogether guilty party.[19]

We live in a world different from that of our fore-
fathers. With the forces of modern society crowding in
upon us, it is necessary that the church today interpret
the Scripture faithfully to mediate love and wholeness to
persons whose marriages have slowly died. Part of our
love will be encouragement to persons to save their marriage if at all possible instead of giving up. Christian love
envisions what the future might hold for persons, and
does not dwell on what the past already produced. The
church today must minister this kind of love.

C. The Church Struggles with the Dangers of Grace

Biblical scholars and pastors who teach a forgiving attitude and generous approach toward divorce may become embroiled in controversy. Persons who emphasize a
more traditional interpretation may lash out against the
"new liberal." Others will wonder when those persons
who call themselves Christians will stop diluting their
own textbook. These persons are campaigning for the
purity of the church, and they wonder how corrupting in-
fluences can produce a clean church. Besides this, forgiving and accepting divorced and remarried persons in the
church will encourage others to follow in the same manner.

Guy Duty lists various objections to a more forgiving
stance on divorce, as posed to him by his own readers.
This objection refers to accommodation and its possible
outcome, and Duty gives his answer:

If we let down the bars, will there not be much abuse of
the remarriage privilege? This objection falsely assumes

that it is scriptural to have bars up in the first place. The scriptures should be dealt with on the basis of what they mean, and not on whether they will be abused. What Bible doctrine or privilege has not been abused?

The privilege of the Fifth Amendment to the U.S. Constitution has been much abused by gangsters . . . but there isn't a court or legislature in America that would abolish it.

Why do non-dissolution churches let down the bars and receive divorced and remarried people into their membership when a minister of another denomination performs the ceremony? And why do they let down the bars to receive the tithes and offerings of divorced-remarried persons? Why do they let down the bars to give them the right to Holy Communion? "Consistency is not only a jewel—it is a rare gem."[20]

Those persons who would hold up the bars do so because they feel the church is set up to be the bulwark of purity. Again, the theological ethic of legalism is meant as a safeguard of that purity. But in the context of divorce and remarriage, these legalists may see mercy in almost the same light as libertinism with both being counter to the church that is truly Christian.

In this context the words of Emil Brunner could fit no better:

Even in matters of marriage God is more merciful than the usual theological ethic, and *to learn to know this mercy of God aright would be a surer means of defense against libertinism than the legalism which so proudly plumes itself upon its "seriousness" and its "freedom from compromise."* Were it not for the fact that pastoral practice has at times acted with far more insight than the official doctrine would have permitted, the disaster would have supervened much earlier. It is the curse of "Christian morality" that it always regards the most legalistic view as the "most serious"[21] (Emphasis mine)

The Church as an Expression of Forgiveness

Those who would "hold the line" regarding divorce and remarriage may feel that to do otherwise is a breaking of the law. But in dealing with divorce the Scripture permits it as a means of acknowledging the law's failure. The law still stands, seasoned by grace.

In fact, the cross is the supreme evidence of God's awareness that man is helpless under the law, and therefore He was willing to make a provision for breaking it. God willingly allowed the death of His Son to keep His own law from sending us to hell. And with this act He brought grace and forgiveness potentially for all, because all of us have broken the law.

Preserving the purity of the church in the question of marital relations can have more effect if a positive approach is taken. Using a negative approach—laws again—puts a veil over purity. For example, prohibiting divorce does not necessarily result in purity. Rather, strong teaching on marriage—its permanence, its values, expectations, and responsibilities—will produce a church closer to the ideal. A strong counseling program, marriage enrichment weekends, periodic preaching on the home, and classes on the young person and sex may be some methods to use. Congregations might plan activities in the home to strengthen family life. However, some persons may still maintain that divorce only remains the sin—not the lack of vital teaching for discipleship that may have contributed to it.

The ideal is to preserve the purity of the church—not allowing the world to squeeze us into its mold with its lifestyle and values. Concessions in marriage may appear, but does not the grace of God as seen in Scripture, allow for them? The church can take the risk because God took the risk to meet the physical, emotional, and

151

spiritual needs of men and women crying out for help.

One of the dangers of such an approach, as noted by Bernard Ramm, is that "any concession for a worthy cause is capitalized upon by an endless number of unworthy persons. The special concession for an aggravated case is turned into an excuse by people whose situation is not aggravated."[22] Some churches believe that if divorce takes place among its members, public confession is necessary to demonstrate to others its seriousness. This in itself may help divert others from divorce. This approach, however, views a case of divorce more as teaching a lesson to the congregation than responsiveness to personal need. And it may even be used as a whipping post of punishment or in some cases produces grist for gossip.

Other churches may capitalize on similar methods of social pressure as their main teaching against divorce. Along with public confession, such measures as refusing remarriage to take place within the church sanctuary, keeping divorced-remarried persons from membership, and denial of positions of leadership to divorced persons all are staged as signs that this is the most serious of sins. One pastor shared with me that he refuses to perform second marriages, and to his knowledge, no one in his church has been married twice. He said, "If we knowingly did this, the youth would think it doesn't matter." He does indicate, however, that never has a divorced person been denied membership or been released from membership. Persons who have divorced while they have been members, desiring remarriage, do not stay around.

The church does need to relate to divorced persons seriously. Persons who live in a society where the "quickie" divorce often takes place need to discover within the church that divorce and remarriage cannot be taken lightly. Today "many, out of pure emotionalism, out of unrealistic impulsiveness (whether over anger, sex attraction, jealousy, pride, or inability to relate caringly) bail out of a fairly livable marriage only to find that singleness is not quite as blissful as they had heard. . . ."[23] And yet I do not think the church should deny (or try to deny) a legal divorce. Using negative measures against the persons who could not maintain their marriage covenant is not the Christian way to teach the sanctity of marriage. Positive steps need to be taken to provide for weak marriages (some of which may already have gone through an internal divorce) if the church is to fulfill its mission. Too often negative dealings that congregations have had with separated or divorced persons communicate open rejection. How can these persons learn love when hit with this reaction after they have gone through such a turmoil of bitterness and enmity? Not only has there been resentment and embitterment against the spouse, but anger and a certain animosity against oneself. The church needs to be present with God's agape love, uplifting, upholding, and caring.

William Cole provides some helpful words to sum this up:

> The church needs desperately to provide the sort of atmosphere where couples with conflicts can come for trained and sympathetic assistance. They do not want or need moralizing sermons at such a time, but most of all an impartial and objective listener. Such a positive approach to preparing people for good marriages and then helping them to maintain their union through storm and stress will go a long way toward rendering the negative wails about divorce obsolete and unnecessary.[24]

D. The Church Accepts Divorced Persons as Members

Any guilt a pastor may feel when he reaches out in the acceptance and the mediation of forgiveness toward a divorcee is accented when he calls for congregational support of his action within the fellowship of the church. In fact, if the congregation as a whole feels this guilt and has not fully resolved its stand, divorced-remarried persons applying for membership may need to work through a maze of negative feelings emitted to them by congregational members.

One fact is true—the pastor must know where he stands. He must have the spiritual and psychological resources to draw from to explain why he takes such a position. And he needs skill to relate to congregational members who have a knack for proof-texting and who can quickly list examples to support a rigid view.

One thing he must deal with is the approach held among some conservative groups and scattered persons who say that before church membership can be offered, remarried persons need to separate and go back to their spouse, or live in an unmarried state.

Arguments to support this belief are set forth in a discussion paper prepared to articulate different views by John R. Mumaw, past president of Eastern Mennonite College, Harrisonburg, Virginia.

(1) Remarriage constitutes a state of adultery which therefore makes their living together a state of sin.

(2) The purity of a believers' church requires the application of this limitation of church membership.

(3) Concessions in this area open the way for compromise of practice in other areas of discipleship.

(4) A modified position will lead eventually to an open door to all kinds of divorce applicants.

(5) Solving this problem by means of relaxation only invites more problems in this and other areas of church life.[25]

Then presenting the opposite view, Mumaw lists reasons that are advanced for extending church membership to persons involved in divorce. He points out, however, that this relaxed view should extend only to those persons involved in divorce *before* conversion. This approach, colored by that concept, argues that—

(1) This state of marriage is not a state of living in sin since the persons so involved have repented, found forgiveness, and are pledged to purity of life in the second marriage.

(2) The approach of Jesus was not legalistic but expressed desire to save the person and that therefore we should be more concerned with saving people than in keeping a rule.

(3) Requiring separation creates more problems than it solves, thus destroying more values than it creates.

(4) Since we do not have a perfect church in other respects it is inconsistent to hold the requirements of separation even though the remarried state may not be the Christian ideal.

(5) Adultery in physical contact and in the lustful look upon another dissolves the marriage bond so that the innocent partner is free to have another marriage.

(6) The realization of forgiveness for the sins of divorce and remarriage qualifies one so involved for acceptance into the fellowship of the church.[26]

All of these points are basic to a rationale for acceptance and assimiliation. Only number one seems to relate specifically to a divorce followed by a conversion, but this could be interpreted to relate to a Christian who may divorce and then seek forgiveness again.

The pastor as a counselor needs to lead his congregation to a full awareness that within the will of God it is possible to extend full membership to persons who have been divorced. Whether the divorce took place before or after conversion is an irrelevant point. In either case he can find forgiveness by God and therefore inclusion within His kingdom. However, the church needs to ask, "How can this acceptance into church membership best be accomplished? Should the church look at alternatives regarding the process of receiving divorced members? How can the pastor be of assistance in this?"

Within the context of a group selected by a local congregation which I assisted, work recently was done concerning policymaking regarding this issue. Listed below are some of the alternatives we considered as a direction for the church.

(1) Do not allow any divorced-remarried persons within the fellowship of the church. On this basis it is intended that a pure church be built. This position looks at divorce and remarriage as an unpardonable sin. By taking this view the church is saying that it is better to bypass such people, because then one does not have to face up to numerous unpleasant problems. Possibly there is some other church which would accept such wrecked lives. Perhaps they could be assimilated in a "less perfect" church.

(2) Allow baptism to be administered to divorced and remarried persons and let them fellowship around the communion table, but do not allow them membership in the church. This may be seen as a compromise position. In this way they can fellowship with the believers, but because they are "less righteous" than other believers their lack of membership will keep them from serving in

church offices or in exercising the right to help make decisions regarding the ongoing life of the church.

(3) Allow associate membership, but because of the past sin, restrict the person to minor offices in the church. Leadership in the congregation can make it quite clear that voting privileges are not offered to such persons.

(4) Another alternative is to decide within the congregation a position or policy for each type of case, with the understanding that the church will abide by these positions in all subsequent situations. For instance these various positions could be taken: "If a man has been single but has married a divorced lady, then . . ." or "If a person is divorced but not remarried, then we advise . . ." or "If a person has been a Christian, but she then becomes separated from her husband because he has been involved in adultery with another woman, then we recommend that to retain church membership, the Christian lady. . . ." In broken marital relationships there are numerous possible combinations of variables—Christian or non-Christian, divorce or separation, remaining single or remarrying, adultery of one or adultery of both—and the like. This alternative, then would run all like cases through the same "computer," and except for the drawing up of the initial policy, the answers could be arrived at quite simply and quickly.

(5) Decide each case on its own merit. For example, when a couple, either or both of whom have been divorced and remarried, apply for church membership, the whole congregation would consider whether they should become a part of the fellowship. They would strive toward consensus concerning the answer. Other cases, such as those cited in No. 4 above, would also be looked at individually, with the persons involved given a certain

amount of subjective consideration.

This gives more personalized attention to a decision that affects the whole spiritual and emotional future of the persons involved. Even though this process has been used with good results, the success of this approach depends upon two factors: (a) The composition of the congregation. Is the congregation composed of persons who tend to be rigid and inflexible in their thinking? Is there a high trust level between individuals? Are persons free as a whole to communicate their feelings and convictions to each other without fear of being intimidated? (b) The emotional stability of the persons being reviewed. It can be detrimental to some persons to be "put on the block," especially if they tend toward paranoia, neurosis, or other kinds of emotional weakness. And if the congregation ends up taking a position of nonacceptance, what effect will this long process have on the couple?

(6) Take such persons into membership only if they appear before the church body in specific confession regarding their divorce and remarriage. The rationale behind this approach is to offer the persons a chance to clear up this past wrong within the body of the congregation. This may also act as a deterrent to others. Younger persons are shown that the church looks upon divorce as wrong, and other married persons see that the church does not condone a quick and easy divorce without restitution in the life of the congregation. This approach poses the problem of placing this one sin in a notorious category which must evoke confession, while sins of worry, hatred, grudges, lying, and materialism, need not be confessed publicly. But even though the church realizes that God has forgiven the persons, it seems almost to be holding a whip over their heads, trying to get

its last licks in by forcing them through the ordeal of confessing in public. And furthermore, some less understanding congregational members may respond only with, "I'm glad I don't have to go through that experience." Others may give evidence of self-righteous pride or of enjoying hearing about the sins of others. Some may even use the occasion as an excuse for gossip.

One divorced person shared with me that she was requested to make such a public confession. Doing this would have guaranteed her continued membership. However, she declined because, as she told me, "I didn't feel it was the whole church's business." In this case she was allowed to retain her membership anyway, but only through a special plea by her parents, who were leaders in the church.

(7) Take divorced-remarried persons into membership on the same basis as any other person. Each congregation has specific requirements for church membership which have evolved through oral tradition, or are delineated in a church constitution. This approach assesses this wrong as no different from any other sin, but instead offers forgiveness and extends acceptance and assimilation within the congregation.

(8) Accept the divorced-remarried person where they are, stress the permanency of marriage as God's divine ideal, and help them resolve guilt feelings through repentance and confession to God and to those they have wronged. Integration within the life of the congregation is most fair for persons if they know specifically what the Bible teaches on moral issues, and what the church attempts to practice. It is important for the pastor to share biblical teaching and special resources on specifics that apply to the case at hand. On the basis of this input, each

applicant should be allowed to judge for himself his own commitment, and suggest his own solutions in becoming an active part of the church membership and Christ's kingdom.

He needs to be led toward a "realized forgiveness" as James Emerson, Jr., suggests. If guilt still persists the pastor on a one-to-one basis can attempt to lead the individual toward a knowledge and awareness of his genuine guilt and the offer of forgiveness from God. Emerson says, "The experience of realizing forgiveness is the positive dimension that makes one free from bondage to a past guilt."[27] If the pastor focuses on the specific marital problem of the applicant and the person's deepest feelings about it, this person may be able to resolve his own feelings and enter into church life with a feeling of newness and deep commitment.

I personally see this last alternative as the most tenable, understanding, and helping approach. The church is assisting such a person in charting a course for the future. As long as he continues to exercise a genuine desire for the blessing of the Lord and His renewing grace within his life, he will be able to find a deeper sense of fulfillment and compatibility with his second spouse.

One danger, as perceived by some, regarding receiving divorced and remarried persons as members is that the church's witness regarding the permanency of marriage is impaired. Even in the process of forgiving and receiving such persons the church needs to stand without apology for the purity of morals and maintain a witness regarding the sanctity of the institution of marriage.

Time may be spent in pastor-to-person counseling on such things as how the breaking of the marriage vow strikes at the foundations of our social structure. It may be helpful to draw attention to the relationship of Christ and the church as an analogy of the husband-wife bond. But even more important than emphasizing theological concepts, persons who have been guilt-laden must be led to true repentance, forgiveness, and the need of a genuine commitment to Christ. Finding healing in Christ will provide the best possible basis for these persons to grow together in building a deep, lasting, and permanent relationship.

This willingness to receive divorced and remarried persons, obviously, is set in the sphere of grace. In opting for this approach, the church is reaching after the lesser of two evils, as it were. The divine ideal is not divorce and remarriage. But the divine ideal also is not a banishment or an ostracizing in this life of those who desire to experience a guilt-ridding, spiritual cleansing—a clean slate on which to begin a new life of faithfulness.

Since we are in the realm of grace, we can make that choice. It is only in the presence of grace, never in the presence of law, that we can speak of "the lesser of two evils."

Dwight Small points out:

> In the sphere of grace, conflicting values must at times be weighed and a discriminating, difficult choice made. How much greater is the difficulty of decision in the sphere of grace, how searching the motivation of the one making such decisions! Yet under the governance of grace, the good of the individual or couple is more than a mere matter of legal arrangement.[28]

How much easier it is for a congregation to say, "He was a Christian; he should have known better," than to sweat through all the implications of the case. How much simpler to quote the letter of either the Old or the New Testament as a standard or measure of personal righteousness than allowing God to look at the heart. At best, human judgments are wide of the mark, for only God knows what is really happening inside a person.

Christians who take a rigid view on divorce and remarriage and see the Bible as a rule book are often guilty themselves of breaking rules regarding judging, showing trust, and displaying love. It has been the tendency throughout history to label the sins that are more visible and tangible as the worse sins. Failing to give evidence of the fruit of the Spirit (Galatians 5:22, 23) does not get Christians in trouble with other Christians nearly as quickly as other "more blatant" sins.

With all the divergence of belief in our churches in respect to law and grace, in regards to the Bible as a rule book or as containing divine operating principles, extending the right hand of fellowship to divorced persons may be a big step. And when a pastor chooses that alternative—acceptance and forgiveness—he may need to spend more time counseling the seasoned members of his congregation than the person caught in the marital problem! It is important that he counsel in love and preach with force what the heart of the church is.

In a survey which I completed in the Mennonite Church—I found that most congregations have not decided upon a policy. Two questions I asked were, "Does your congregation retain as members persons who are divorced and remarried?" and "Does your church receive new members who have been divorced and remarried?" It was striking to discover answers like, "We have not had the experience," or "We have no such cases." Other answers were, "We have not been faced with this decision," and "We have no set policy at this time." In response to these, I would ask, "How fast could your church reach such a decision if you were thrust into such a situation? Would a divorced and remarried applicant for membership in your church have enough ego-strength to persist through the whole decision-making process?" Possibly some would but others would not.

In one situation a family in which the wife had been divorced but now was remarried applied for church membership, and the church at this time had no policy statement. The pastor discerned the situation and encouraged the church to accept her, and then do an in-depth study of divorce and remarriage. "But the church would not budge," he writes. "We did the study, decided to accept her, but by then she was gone—hurt *very badly*." She was threatened so much by the delay and the discussion that she stopped coming. "It was a case where we lost a person in order to meet the church's need," the pastor states.

An example such as this should encourage all congregations to make a decision on what they believe on the divorce-remarriage issue even though they have not presently faced it. Some pastors, in answer to my questionnaire, felt that they would tend in the direction of receiving divorced-remarried persons as members. One said, "I feel we would give strong consideration." This leniency is commendable, but it would be far more helpful for these congregations and the pastors to determine beforehand their approach to such cases. And it would, no doubt, be more redemptive and less fearful for the persons being considered for membership.

As we look into the developing New Testament church, we find that this question also had to be faced.

From the Pauline Epistles we discover that in certain instances the church accepted the marriage situation as it was, and then applied to it Christian standards and Christian values. The New Testament saints lived in a wicked and perverse society, similar to ours today. Theirs was an immoral, degraded, and lost generation. Corinth was the epitome of debauchery. Paul does not mince any words in speaking about the evils of this wicked seaport city. In 1 Corinthians 5 he mentions a case of incest. In the sixth chapter, after naming specific sexual sins of fornication, adultery, and homosexuality among other sins, Paul reminds the believers that such were some of them. The next chapter deals almost exclusively with marriage problems and ends with this statement: "So, dear brothers, whatever situation a person is in when he becomes a Christian, let him stay there, for now the Lord is there to help him" (1 Corinthians 7:24, *The Living Bible*).

The pastor plays a leading role in setting attitudes and directing the process of accepting into membership persons from broken marriages. He needs to preach a "Come as you are" message. This is the picture of Christ that the church must present. C. S. Lovett put it this way:

> What a horrible inconsistency to say, "Come," and then throw up a barricade of thorns in the path of those with unfortunate marriage records. How many families have suffered hurt because of this ungracious procedure. . . . The story is even more unlovely when the divorced person shares an equal status with the gossipers, the hot-tempered deacons and elders, and the critical church gatherers. . . . The pastor who can marry the ex-murderer and the wiretapper, admitting them to church office, can with equal conscience marry and even remarry divorced individuals.[29]

Possibly in the past the church has had its priorities misarranged in preaching forgiveness for all the sins that cause the death of the marriage but failing to preach forgiveness for the death itself. Sins of hostility, resentment, silence, impatience, bitterness, and pride have kept growing and growing until they were impossible to handle, and the marriage died. As Hudson says, "They get divorces, not over one felonious assault, but over minute misdemeanors which would be better overlooked."[30]

The church has often sanctioned a marriage just because it had been legally contracted. Until a marriage is legally divorced, we like to think that it is still fulfilling God's plan of holy matrimony. The individuals are considered to be "one flesh," although this may no longer be the case. The church which finds it so difficult to recognize and accept a legal divorce has many times passively sat by while an internal divorce was in existence for many years.

Dwight Small writes:

> When marriage fails to become a catalyst for human personality, the normal road to full self-realization, then marriage as intended does not exist. Or when marriage creates and sustains loneliness, and supplants integration of persons with disintegration, it is bereft of its essential meaning. While two people may continue to live alongside each other, enacting all the familiar marital rituals, the marriage itself may be dead. . . . No formal contractual recognition can make of this a marriage; internal divorce has already taken place and simply awaits formal recognition.[31]

Some Christians say, "I can't get a divorce because I am a Christian. I don't believe in divorce." What they may really be saying is that they do not believe in legal or civil divorce. Without question they believe in divorce because they have allowed themselves to be internally divorced. They have been divorced from each other in the sight of God. Before the church allows itself to take such a strong unyielding position against civil divorce, it would do well to understand this paradox, and do more to prevent internal divorces.

With all of this before us, what rule, then, can we adopt in accepting persons into membership? Bernard Ramm points out that the "rule of redemption" must be foremost. He says, "The church ought to follow ethical policies that are redemptive, that are healing, that offer hope for happiness in the future, and that do not intend to harm or hurt people simply to comply with the ethics of their 'in group.' "[32]

Pastors today need to lead their churches toward a new sense of compassion, mercy, and redemption. It is important that they help their people understand the tragedy of divorce. There are so many complexities that simplistic answers point up a person's naivetée. If the church can redeem these persons and open doors of hope to them, they will find new life. If the church does not, they will be plunged further into deeper despair and deeper problems.

E. The Church Personifies Forgiveness to Its People

In many respects, being divorced is not the easy way out. On their own admission, often neither spouse realized the shattering experience that living with divorce would bring to them. As one divorced woman said, "It's just like a death in the family. It's a loneliness you can't fill. You've just got to live with it."

Divorce is a trauma similar to bereavement. Both involve status change, loss of spouse, economic difficulties, and sexual deprivation. Probably the divorced person undergoes much more personal disorganization than the widow in that the widow generally obtains social support and has a well-defined role to play.

The emotional attachment of divorcing spouses is less than that of partners whose marriage ends through death. This makes the death separation more traumatic, and yet other inner dynamics are present in the case of divorce. The person facing a marriage breakup generally over the months was "being divorced." During this time he struggled with deep feelings of bitterness, conflict, hostility, loneliness, and misfortune. Even though both partners may have agreed to terminate their marriage, these feelings will persist for years to come. God's grace and love can minister in this situation so that bitterness and hostility are gradually healed as time goes on. But the feeling of loneliness and isolation can become greater and greater.

Many times the church, community, social organizations, and sometimes even the families of divorced persons begin to treat these persons as outcasts. One person said, "I now know what it's like to be a minority person. You don't really fit in any group and people look at you as being different. For the first time in my life I can identify with black people."[33]

In conducting personal interviews with divorced persons, I discovered this sense of rejection. One person said, "I had that 'black sheep' feeling and I stopped going to church. I seemed to be in limbo and was definitely segregated. However, persons who were my closer friends before remained friends afterwards."

Another woman said, "Some friends were true, but my

feeling of isolation was much my own fault. I drew into a shell. I felt a lack of acceptance, but I don't know how much of it was myself or the people. . . . A divorcee must go through a certain period before she can feel integrated again." In this case one person did show strong support and gestures of kindness. "She would just listen," the divorcee exclaimed, "and that's just what I needed at the time." She reflected a moment, then added, "Just recently people have reached out to me. They couldn't beforehand because of the wall I had built around myself."

Another divorced person said she experienced a feeling of identity and understanding when she was able to share conversation with another divorcee. This helped tremendously to bring her out of her shell.

It is important that the pastor himself reaches out immediately in support of the divorced individual. "The pastor may only give a pat on the back, and that can help," one person commented. Another person cautioned, "The pastor should not push the divorcee, but make it clear that he is there. . . . I felt a need to unload to the pastor, but didn't feel free to talk to him at the time."

"I began feeling human again when I began doing work in the church, even though it was menial work," one person said. "When I was forced to be with people, it was then I felt a part of the congregation. It is important to do things with people."

Since partners who decide to split up cannot simply walk out of each other's lives without carrying heartaches, bad feelings, spells of anxiety, and a continual rehashing of the past, the church needs to step in with open arms to relate to these persons. Ramm points out that "any couple contemplating divorce must realize that the legal end of a marriage and the emotional ending of a marriage are two very different things and to think that they both happen at the same time is part of the tragedy of the divorce phenomenon."[34]

Too often churches contribute to many of these negative factors which a member had to face by ostracizing such a person or eyeing him with suspicion. "Because of the traumatic experience of divorce and the social stigma attached, there is a tendency for the divorcee who is suffering from an emotional disturbance to have the disturbance increased."[35]

How can a pastor help his church in ministering to the needs of persons suffering deeply from broken relationships?

(1) The pastor should build within the congregation a tenable position on which persons can stand. Many Christian leaders have chosen to ignore this controversial subject. One man said, "I have been a Christian for forty-seven years and have not heard one sermon on divorce." A minister of seventeen years' experience admitted he had never preached on the topic though he has definite views.[36]

No doubt many people shy away from divorced persons because they have a host of unanswered questions about the biblical teaching on divorce. John R. Martin says, "Many of us would be willing to relate to them and hurt with them if *our* ethical questions were answered."[37] If we bring this subject out in the open, and give sound biblical teaching and practical application on it, congregational members will feel more at ease about how to handle it. This will help foster an atmosphere for dialogue and caring.

(2) If the pastor-counselor can share with couples and

his congregation that there are actually two kinds of divorce—internal divorce and civil divorce—this can help change the perspective toward divorce. Internal divorce takes place in homes where all kinds of conflict and resentment are present, where there may really be a dead marriage, and yet both spouses live under the same roof. A pastor will help his members consider the quality of their own homes and not focus only on the problems of others. One writer says, "Rather than pointing his accusing finger at a brother with a civil divorce record, the discriminator may look at himself and ask, 'Is there really a true heart union between my wife and myself? Is ours a marriage in God's eyes or is it a mask for the eyes of our brothers? Am I myself a spiritual divorcee?' "[38]

If a pastor as a counselor to his people deliberately works at strengthening family life in his church, he will help prevent marital crack-ups and assist post-divorced persons to build their second marriage on the solid rock of Christ. He may arrange for stronger families in his church to befriend couples who are having difficulties. He needs also to encourage couples to seek counseling when the marital road becomes rocky.

(3) The pastor can help the divorced person to develop new relationships. Besides losing a spouse during the family breakup one may experience the loss of children, friends, or even a job. Relationships formed over the years are suddenly terminated. The person is isolated and alone. Where can he form new relationships? Some go to the local bar. Others may choose the church.

As a basis for encouraging new one-to-one relationships, the church needs by all means to extend understanding love to persons in this predicament and the assurance of a sense of brotherhood. Divorced individuals need the support of fellowship and a continuing interest in their problem. Sharing concern and fellowship can diminish the persons' sense of seclusion.

In showing fellowship and acceptance the pastor needs help from many persons. To build new relationships he can offer suggestions of groups or clubs where the divorced ones can rebuild a circle of friends.

Possibly groups could be formed also such as "Parents Without Partners' where members of one or more local congregations could get together, discuss, and find solutions to the problems of loneliness, lack of finances, and the like. The church could also refer them to a "Parents Without Partners" chapter. Local chapters of this national organization are organized as interest and needs arise. Often they have a professional person such as a pastoral counselor or a social worker to talk on a subject followed by open discussion and mutual sharing of problems divorce brings, such as loneliness, discipline of children, and church expectations.

(4) The pastor can encourage full participation within the life of the congregation. If the pastor accepts and attempts to assimilate the divorced person into the life of the church, church members too will reach out their hands to them despite the circumstances and reasons for the divorce. Marion Steiner points out that "as the church invites the divorcee to participate in such sacraments as the Lord's Supper, the church is reinforcing the fact that not only does God forgive but fellow members are also being forgiving and are standing by to help the divorcee experience forgiveness."[39]

One of the alternatives concerning the requirements or procedure for church membership is that of acceptance as "associate members." In this case they are not allowed fully to participate in the ministry and organizational procedures of the church. However, since the church of Jesus Christ consists not only of the pure but of those being purified, the pastor needs to encourage that persons with gifts be used in the church. Many times persons caught in the web of divorce have not been allowed to hold offices in the church, and consequently that person's gifts have lain idle and wasted away.

God's program is big enough to accommodate both the divorced and the non-divorced Christian. William L. Coleman says, "The divorced person is very unlikely to corrupt the people in the church by his conduct or his doctrine. Often he is far more tender and caring because of the tragedy he has experienced. He is a member of the body of Christ—one of those eyes, ears, feet, or hands that Paul told us about."[40]

(5) The pastor should encourage social service when needed. There are times when financial assistance is needed by a divorced person and providing this shows caring and warmth. When the divorced person is a woman, members could offer to assist in performing the usual household mechanical repairs. Periodically arrangements could be made to provide babysitting services to relieve the mother for an evening. If she needs to be employed outside the home, the church may look into the possibility of providing day-care services for the children.

The pastor can encourage the kinds of ministries to divorced persons mentioned above through his own attitude and action toward divorced persons. His example will carry his words deep into the hearts of his parishioners. His pulpit ministry can enhance what he shares with his congregation on a one-to-one basis. Pastors verbally must continue to encourage that members include divorced persons in sincere, nonjudgmental fellowship. A special effort should be made to reassure such persons that we are not angry at them, we are not afraid of them, and our fellowship is open to them.

F. The Church Assists in Remarriages

According to Andrew Eickhoff, persons contemplating remarriage should be helped by the Christian church in the following ways:

(1) Toward an understanding of their responsibility for the failure in the first marriage.
(2) Toward a sufficient interval to permit adjustment and full acceptance of this responsibility so that divorce will not happen again.
(3) Toward the firm commitment of the person to establish, this time, a Christian home.[41]

The pastor, because of his position, needs to take the initiative in the implementation of these principles. Hopefully, his congregation can agree with him that these are valid for the remarriage of divorced persons. Possibly he will want to test them out with his congregation. It will be helpful to him as he personally relates to the couple contemplating remarriage to know his congregation is behind him in his effort in the couple's behalf.

It is said that 90 percent of the persons desiring marriage prefer to have a ceremony performed by a minister. And it has also been discovered that 90 percent of those who are divorced remarry. Therefore the church could potentially be involved in marrying many divorced persons.

The pastor's decision to marry a couple, is an important one. His decision indicates that he feels the persons have the potential for a successful marriage. It is important, therefore, that a pastor assess the maturity of the couple who comes to him for marriage. When remarriage is involved this is more significantly true.

As in premarital counseling, the pastor needs to share with the couple some basic principles again. Marriage vows are for "as long as we both shall live." The living out of these vows for the Christian couple involves a relationship with self, family, and the church. Can the couple face these relationships with confidence?[42]

In this counseling the pastor needs to sense if the divorced person carries any guilt from his former marriage. The remarriage may be looked upon as an attempt to overcome some guilt, but after the newness of the marriage is past, the sense of guilt may return, and then the person may have difficulty living with himself and his spouse. Again it comes back to the concept of a "realized forgiveness."

Another point to consider here is the minister's own feelings about his relationship to this kind of situation. Emerson says, "If the minister felt guilty about his relationship to the situation how could he hope to mediate forgiveness to the couple?"[43]

If a pastor is bound by his own feelings of guilt, his ability to minister to the couple in premarital counseling, in performing the ceremony, and in relating to the family afterward will be weak.

The pastor in sharing with the couple seeking remarriage needs to ask them about their feeling of acceptance from the congregation. Since the marriage covenant is seen as relating to community, Christian marriage should be a congregational experience. John R. Martin says:

> The witnesses to the marriage should include some who
> will worship with them after marriage. Acceptance by the
> congregation is most important where there has been re-
> marriage. Members of a congregation who do not feel ac-
> ceptance will not become a vital part of the fellowship.[44]

Andrew Eickhoff expresses well the attitude of an accepting congregation when he says that "the church
members must be readied to accept divorced persons and
those remarried in the church as repentant sinners who
deserve a second chance and the support of the community in Christian love."[45]

As stated earlier the pastor needs to face his congregation with this challenge: "Is the church able to minister
to the needs of people where they are? How does the
church apply its doctrine of forgiveness? How can the
church make people involved in marriage irregularities
be made to feel loved and understood?"

John R. Mumaw in an unpublished manuscript says,
"In dealing with remarriage of divorced persons we face
issues that are concerned with the very nature of the
church and its mission. In one sense the question of remarriage forces us to reexamine the relevancy of the
Christian faith in resolving human problems."[46] How
can the pastor best get this truth across to his congregation?

Some Christians today feel that their church is most
godly when it has plateaued above human error and impurity. However, if the stance could ever be attained
their "church" would cease being *the church* because its
whole sense of mission would be lost. It would have become a failure in fulfilling its divinely appointed role,

and would only stand as a showcase for "saints" instead of a hospital for those with human ills.

It is evidenced in the Scripture that forgiveness stands at the very heart of the gospel and therefore needs to predominate in the life and mission of the church. Because of this fact the congregation that wishes to carry out God's unswerving purpose must take a serious look at the responsibility it has for divorced persons—and even for those who wish to consider remarriage.

In some respects it is only within the context of the Christian faith that remarriage (after divorce) can be made theologically justifiable and actually practical. Within the circle of the congregation, with help from pastor and people, two persons who wish to make a reentry into a satisfying and successful marital bond, can hopefully find a strong footing. Such a foundation may not be possible if they are pushed away from the spiritual vitality of the congregation.

The faithful church affirms its divine calling to the greatest degree when it envisions new victories in persons' lives instead of concentrating on past defeats. The faithful church will engender new successes for the remarried. It will affirm this remarriage as a creative force that does not need to allow minor hindrances to happiness to result in the destruction of another marriage. The faithful church will uphold and encourage permanence in marriage as God's divine will, and yet it will be courageous enough to share His abounding grace!

G. A Summary

In this chapter we have considered some very practical applications of the law-grace motif. How will the congregation deal with these issues in the church pew, the pastor's office, or at the communion table? That is the critical question.

Perhaps the words of Dwight Small are an appropriate summary of the views I have attempted to set forth:

> Let the Church be bold in grace! Let the divorced and re-married feel fully accepted in the community of sinners saved by grace! Let the remarried find places of service in the Church alongside those whose experience of the forgiving grace of God concerns less conspicuous areas of life. Let there be no penalties in the Church where God disallows such penalties. Let there be a recognition of the necessity for the tragic moral choice in this world, the necessity, at times, of choosing the lesser of two evils. Let us rejoice that the absolute will of God is not compromised, but that He conditions the exercise of His will to our imperfect faith and obedience, to our sins and our failures. And may the knowledge of such great grace fill our minds and hearts with such responding love as will motivate us to attempt in every way to fulfill His highest will in the power of enabling grace![47]

Notes: Chapter IV

1. Jane Lamb, "Alone/Responsible," *Christian Home*, March 1972, p. 8.

2. *Ibid.*, p. 11.

3. Otto A. Piper, "Broken Family in the Bible," *Pastoral Psychology*, December 1967, p. 18.

4. Wes Bryan, "Divorce Is Writing a Chapter That Doesn't Fit," *Christian Living*, January 1975, p. 18.

5. Bernard L. Ramm, *The Right, the Good, and the Happy* (Waco, Tex.: Word Books, 1971), p. 88.

6. Maynard Shelly, ed., *Studies in Church Discipline* (Newton, Kan.: Mennonite Publication Office, 1958), p. 149.

7. Peter J. Dyck, Task Force on Divorce, Remarriage, and Church Membership, Akron (Pa.) Mennonite Church, September 15, 1974. Used by permission.

Divorce and the Faithful Church

8. Abraham Schmitt, "Divorce—How Jesus Saw It," *Christian Living*, November 1975, p. 20.

9. Wayne E. Oates, *Pastoral Counseling in Social Problems* (Philadelphia: Westminster Press, 1961), pp. 106, 107.

10. Schmitt, *op. cit.*, p. 21.

11. James G. Emerson, Jr., *Divorce, the Church, and Remarriage* (Philadelphia: Westminster Press, 1961), pp. 23, 24.

12. Alvin Toffler, *Future Shock* (New York: Bantam Books, 1970), p. 252.

13. Bryan, *op. cit.*, pp. 16, 17.

14. R. Lofton Hudson, *'Til Divorce Do Us Part* (Nashville: Thomas Nelson, 1973), p. 83.

15. Victor J. Pospishil, *Divorce and Remarriage* (New York: Herder and Herder, 1967), p. 92.

16. C. S. Lovett, *The Compassionate Side of Divorce (Baldwin Park, Calif.: Personal Christianity Publishers, 1975), p. 102.*

17. *H. Richard Niebuhr, Christ and Culture* (New York: Harper and Brothers, 1951), p. 93.

18. Lovett, *op. cit.*, p. 102.

19. William Barclay, *Ethics in a Permissive Society* (New York: Harper and Row, Publishers, 1971), pp. 203, 204.

20. Guy Duty, *Divorce and Remarriage* (Minneapolis: Bethany Fellowship, Inc., 1967), pp. 126, 127.

21. Emil Brunner, *The Divine Imperative* (Philadelphia: Westminster Press, 1947), p. 354.

22. Ramm, *op. cit.*, p. 89.

23. Hudson, *op. cit.*, pp. 92, 93.

24. William Graham Cole, *Sex and Love in the Bible* (New York: Association Press, 1959), p. 340.

25. John R. Mumaw, "Issues in the Problem of Divorce and Remarriage," Study Paper, p. 14.

26. *Ibid.*

27. Emerson, *op. cit.*, p. 24.

28. Dwight Hervey Small, *The Right to Remarry* (Old Tappan, N.J.: Revell, 1975), p. 37.

29. Lovett, *op. cit.*, pp. 141, 142.

30. Hudson, *op. cit.*, p. 13.

31. Small, *op. cit.*, pp. 15, 16.

32. Ramm, *op. cit.*, p. 88.

33. John R. Martin, "Suffering with the Separated and Divorced," *Gospel Herald*, June 10, 1975, p. 430.

34. Ramm, *op. cit.*

35. Marion Steiner, "What It's Like to Be Divorced," *The Program Builder* (Date Unknown), p. 48.

36. William L. Coleman, "Ministering to the Divorced," *Christianity Today*, June 20, 1975, p. 29.

37. Martin, *op. cit.*

38. Lovett, *op. cit.*, p. 137.

39. Marion Steiner, "Attitudes Toward Divorced Persons," *The Program Builder* (Date Unknown), p. 53.

40. Coleman, *op. cit.*, p. 137.

41. Andrew R. Eickhoff, *A Christian View of Sex and Marriage* (New York: Free Press, 1966), p. 211.

42. John R. Martin, *Divorce and Remarriage, A Perspective for Counseling* (Scottdale, Pa.: Herald Press, 1974), p. 123.

43. Emerson, *op. cit.*, p. 25.

44. Martin, *Divorce and Remarriage, op. cit.*, p. 125.

45. Eickhoff, *op. cit.*, p. 212.

46. Mumaw, *op. cit.*, p. 10.

47. Small, *op. cit.*, p. 186.

BIBLIOGRAPHY

Baker's Dictionary of Christian Ethics. Grand Rapids: Baker Book House, 1973.

Barclay, William. *Ethics in a Permissive Society.* New York: Harper and Row, 1971.

Biblia Hebraica. Germany: Wurttembergische Bibellanstalt Stuttgart, 1937.

Book of Discipline of the United Methodist Church, 1976. The. Nashville: The United Methodist Publishing House, 1976.

Book of discipline of the United Methodist Church, 1976, The. Nashville: The United Methodist Publishing House, 1976.

Brown, Frances, Driver, S. R., and Briggs, C. A., *A Critical and Exegetical Commentary on Deuteronomy* in *The International Critical Commentary.* Edinburgh: T. & T. Clark, 1902.

Brunner, Emil. *The Divine Imperative.* Philadelphia: Westminster Press, 1947.

Bullinger, Ethelbert W. *A Critical Lexicon and Concordance to the English and Greek New Testament.* Grand Rapids: Zondervan, 1975.

Buttrick, George Arthur, ed. *The Interpreters Bible,* Vol. II. New York: Abingdon Press, 1953.

———. *The Interpreters Dictionary of the Bible,* Vol. III, IV. New York: Abingdon Press, 1962.

Church of the Brethren Annual Conference, Richmond, Virginia. Elgin, Ill.: Brethren Press, 1977.

Church of the Nazarene Manual 1976. Kansas City, Missouri: Nazarene Publishing House, 1976.

Cole, William Graham. *Sex and Love in the Bible.* New York: Association Press, 1959.

Constitution and Canons, The Episcopal Church, 1973, New York: Seabury Press, 1973

Constitution of the United Presbyterian Church in the United

States of America, Part I, Book of Confessions, The
Philadelphia: The Office of the General Assembly of the
United Presbyterian Church in the United States of
America, 1967.

*Constitution of the United Presbyterian Church in the United
States of America, Part II, Book of Order, The.*
Philadelphia: The Office of the General Assembly of the
United Presbyterian Church in the United States of
America, 1967.

Driver, S. R. *A Critical and Exegetical Commentary on
Deuteronomy* in *The International Critical Commentary.*
New York: Scribner's, 1895.

Driver, S. R., Plummer, A., and Briggs, C. A., *A Critical and
Exegetical Commentary on Deuteronomy of The International Critical Commentary.* Edinburgh: T. & T. Clark,
1902.

Duty, Guy. *Divorce and Remarriage.* Minneapolis: Bethany
Fellowship, 1967.

Eickhoff, Andrew R. *A Christian View of Sex and Marriage.*
New York: Free Press, 1966.

Emerson, James G. *Divorce, the Church, and Remarriage.*
Philadelphia: Westminster Press, 1952.

Groshiede, F. W. *Commentary on the First Epistle to the
Corinthians.* Grand Rapids: Eerdmans, 1953.

Hastings, James, ed. *A Dictionary of the Bible.* New York:
Scribner's, 1899.

_____. *Encyclopaedia of Religion and Ethics,* Vol. VIII. New
York: Scribner's, 1953.

Herbermann, Charles G. *The Catholic Encyclopedia.* New
York: Encyclopedia Press, 1909.

Hudson R. Lofton. *'Til Divorce Do Us Part.* Nashville: Nelson,
1973.

Interlinear Greek-English New Testament (The Nestle Greek
Text). Literal English Translation by Alfred Marshall.
London: Samuel Bagster and Sons Limited, 1959.

Jackson, Samuel Macauley, ed. *Schaff-Herzog Encyclopedia of*

Religious Knowledge. New York: Funk & Wagnalls, 1891.

Kauffman, J. Howard and Harder, Leland. *Anabaptists Four Centuries Later*. Scottdale, Pa.: Herald Press, 1975.

Keil, C. F. and Delitzsch, F. *The Pentateuch* in *The Biblical Commentary of the Old Testament*, Vol. III. Grand Rapids: Eerdmans, 1949.

Kittel, G., Friedrich, Gerhard, ed. *Theological Dictionary of the New Testament*. Grand Rapids: Eerdmans, 1967.

Knight, George A. F. *Law and Grace*. Philadelphia: Westminster Press, 1962.

Lambeth Conference, 1948, The—The Encyclical Letter from the Bishops Together with Resolutions and Reports. New York: Macmillian, 1931.

Lambeth Conference, 1968, The—Resolutions and Reports. New York: Seabury Press, 1968.

Landman, Isaac, ed. *The Universal Jewish Encyclopedia*, Vol. III. New York: Universal Jewish Encyclopedia, 1941.

Lovett, C. S. *The Compassionate Side of Divorce*. Baldwin Park, Calif.: Personal Christianity, 1975.

Luther's Catechism. Philadelphia: United Lutheran Publication House, 1935.

Mace, David R. *Hebrew Marriage*. New York: Philosophical Library, 1953.

Manson, R. W. *The Teachings of Jesus*. Cambridge: Cambridge University Press, 1935.

Manual of the Christian and Missionary Alliance, 1975 Edition. Nyack, N.Y.: The Christian and Missionary Alliance, 1976.

Martin, John R. *Divorce and Remarriage, A Perspective for Counseling*. Scottdale, Pa.: Herald Press, 1974.

Murray, John. *Divorce*. Philadelphia: Committee on Christian Education, The Orthodox Presbyterian Church, 1953.

Nichols, James Hastings. *History of Christianity 1650-1950*. New York: Ronald Press, 1956.

Niebuhr, H. Richard. *Christ and Culture*. New York: Harper and Brothers, 1951.

Bibliography

Oates, Wayne E. *Pastoral Counseling in Social Problems.* Philadelphia: Westminster Press, 1961.

O'Mahoney, Patrick J., ed. *Catholics and Divorce.* London: Thomas Nelson, 1959.

Orr, James, ed. *The International Standard Biblical Encyclopaedia.* Grand Rapids: Eerdmans, 1947.

Parkhurst, John. *A Greek and English Lexicon of the New Testament.* London: Printed for William Baynes and Sons, 1822.

Peters, George W. *Divorce and Remarriage.* Chicago: University Press, 1972.

Pospishil, Victor J. *Divorce and Remarriage.* New York: Herder and Herder, 1967.

Ramm, Bernard L. *The Right, the Good, and the Happy.* Waco, Tex.: Word, 1971.

Report of the Lambeth Conference 1930, Encyclical Letter from the Bishop with Resolutions and Reports. New York: Macmillian, 1931.

Sadler, M. F. *The Epistles to the Corinthians with Notes.* London: George Bell and Sons, 1891.

Schmid, Heinrich. Doctrinal Theology of the Evangelical Lutheran Church. Minneapolis: Augsburg Publishing House, 1961.

Shelly, Maynard, ed. *Studies in Church Discipline.* Newton, Kan.: Mennonite Publication Office, 1958.

Singer, Isadore, ed. *The Jewish Encyclopedia.* New York: Funk and Wagnalls, 1903.

Small, Dwight Hervey. *The Right to Remarry.* Old Tappan, New Jersey: Revell, 1975.

Stott, John R. W. *Divorce.* Downers Grove, Illinois: Inter-Varsity Press, 1973.

Strong, James. *Strong's Concordance.* New York: Abingdon Press, 1963.

Teachings and Practice on Marriage and Divorce. Minneapolis: Commission on Research and Social Action of the American Lutheran Church, 1965.

Divorce and the Faithful Church

Thayer, Joseph Henry. *A Greek-English Lexicon of the New Testament*. New York: American Book Company, 1886.

Toffler, Alvin. *Future Shock*. New York: Bantam Books, 1970.

Trench, Richard Chenevix. *Notes on the Parables of our Lord*. London: Kegan Paul, Trench, Trubner, 1915.

Wenger, John C. *Dealing Redemptively with Those Involved in Divorce and Remarriage Problems*. Scottdale, Pa.: Herald Press, 1968.

———. ed. *The Complete Writings of Menno Simons, c. 1496-1561*. Scottdale, Pa.: Herald Press, 1956.

Winnett, Arthur Robert. *Divorce and Remarriage in Anglicanism*. London: Macmillian, 1958.

Wrenn, Lawrence G., ed. *Divorce and Remarriage in the Catholic Church*. New York: Newman Press, 1973.

Articles and Unpublished Manuscripts

Bryan, Wes. "Divorce Is Writing a Chapter That Doesn't Fit." *Christian Living*, January, 1975.

Coiner, H. G. "Those Divorce-Remarriage Passages." *Concordia Theological Monthly*, June 1968.

Coleman, William L. "Ministering to the Divorced." *Christianity Today*, June 20, 1975.

Detweiler, Richard. "A Biblical Introduction to the Question of Divorce and Remarriage." A sermon preached on June 24, 1973.

Dyck, Peter J. Article used by the Task Force on Divorce, Remarriage, and Church Membership, Akron (Pa.) Mennonite Church, September 15, 1974.

Lamb, Jane. "Alone/Responsible." *Christian Home*, March 1972.

Martin, John R. "Suffering with the Separated and Divorced." *Gospel Herald*, June 10, 1975.

Mumaw, John R. "Issues in the Problem of Divorce and Remarriage." A study paper.

Peterman, Roy J. "Divorce and Remarriage—The Matter of Exegesis and the Question of Hermeneutics." Study

184

Bibliography

paper prepared for the Brethren in Christ study on marriage, divorce, and remarriage.

Piper, Otto A. "Broken Family in the Bible." *Pastoral Psychology*, December 1967.

Schmitt, Abraham. "Divorce—How Jesus Saw It." *Christian Living*, November 1975.

Soulen, Richard N. "Marriage and Divorce—A Problem in New Testament Interpretation." *Interpretation—A Journal of Bible and Theology*, October 1969.

Steiner, Marion. "Attitudes toward Divorced Persons." *The Program Builder* (Date Unknown)

_____ "*What It's Like to Be Divorced.*" *The Program Builder* (Date Unknown)

Wenger, Linden M. "Divorce and Remarriage in the Old Testament." Paper written for a Study Conference on Divorce and Remarriage, April 1961.

INDEX OF
SCRIPTURE REFERENCES

OLD TESTAMENT

NEW TESTAMENT

Index of Scripture References

187

INDEX

General Index

Divorce Act, 81
Divorced
  church membership of, 154-
    166
  guilt felt by, 137, 140, 142,
    154, 174
  innocent-guilty spouse, 70,
    82, 148
  judgment of, 137, 148
  rejection of, 134, 135, 137,
    167
Dowry, 20
Driver, Plummer, & Briggs, 30
Driver, S. R., 22
Duty, Guy, 38-40, 46, 56, 149

Easton, Burton, 126
Eickhoff, Andrew, 173, 175
Emerson, James G., Jr., 71, 72,
    142, 160
Episcopalian approach, 71, 87-
    90
Exception clause, 36, 41-45, 81,
    99, 147
Excommunication, 100

Fall, The, 18, 124
Foley, W. M., 41, 47
Forgiveness, 49, 50, 61, 136,
    142, 160
Fornication, 31, 41-43; 45, 46,
    48, 79

God
  commands of, 50
  forgiveness of, 136, 138, 139,
    142
  grace of, 126, 127
  intent for marriage by, 16-18,
    38, 60
  love of, 123
  perfect will of, 61
Grace, 49, 122-127, 129, 161
  by church, 18
  dangers of, 149, 153
Guilt, 154

Harrelson, W. J., 118
Hillel, 29, 30, 37
Horst, Irvin B., 75
Hudson, R. Loften, 144

Innocent party, 86, 90, 95
Internal divorce, 109, 146, 165,
    166, 170
Israel, 116, 117

Jewish marriage, 19, 20

Kauffman, J. Howard, and Le-
    land Harder, 107, 108
Keil, C. F., and F. Delitzch, 22
Kierkegaard, Sören, 147
Knight, George A. F., 116, 117

Lambert of Avignon, 76
Lambeth Conferences, 68, 82-
    85
Law, 53, 115-122, 128-131
Legalism, 108, 150
Lord Jowitt, 82
Lovett, C. S., 119, 146, 148, 164
Luther, Martin, 74-76, 90
Lutheran Church, 90-92

Mace, David, 24
Manson, T. W., 121
Marriage
  annulment, 43, 74, 78, 81,
    85, 88-90
  binding relationship, 53, 57,
    80, 101
  church assisting in, 103, 151
  civil law, 69, 78
  dissolution of, 39-41, 59, 61,
    92
  divine ideal, 17, 18, 51, 117,
    118, 137, 159, 161
  Jewish, 19, 20
  loving relationship, 120
  monogamous, 16, 60, 84
  one flesh, 17
  peace in, 60

189

General Index

Trinity Mennonite Church, 106

Unpardonable sin, 49, 97, 108, 156

Wenger, John C., 20, 32, 48, 104

Winnett, A. R., 85
Wismar Articles, 104
Women in the Old Testament, 34
Wordsworth, Bishop, 58
Wynn, John Charles, 97

Mike Parsons Photo

G. Edwin Bontrager is pastor of the Santa Ana Church of the Brethren in Santa Ana, California.

A native of Williamsville, New York, he received his DMin degree from Fuller Theological Seminary in 1976 with specialization in marriage and family counseling, his BD degree from Eastern Mennonite Seminary in 1966, and his BA degree from Eastern Mennonite College in 1963.

Following his graduation from EMS he served the college as admissions counselor and as assistant pastor of the Trissels Mennonite Church, Broadway, Virginia. Moving to northern Ohio he became Bible instructor at Central Christian High School, Kidron, and served as pastor at the Pleasant View Mennonite Church, North Lawrence, for seven years. Along with his studies at Fuller beginning in 1974, he assisted on the ministerial staff at the Seventh Street Mennonite Church, Upland, California.

Bontrager and his wife, Edie, are the parents of two daughters, Andrea and Michele.